HEAVENLY PLACES
REVEALED

A THIRTY-ONE DAY DEVOTIONAL GUIDE TO EPHESIANS

ALLEN SATTERLEE

CREST
BOOKS

Copyright © 2024 by The Salvation Army

Published by Crest Books

Crest Books
The Salvation Army National Headquarters
615 Slaters Lane
Alexandria, VA 22314
Phone: 703-684-5523

Lt. Colonel Lesa Davis, Editor-in-Chief
Caleb Louden, Managing Editor
Maryam Outlaw, Editorial Assistant

Andrea Martin, Graphic Designer

ISBN print: 978-1-946709-29-5

Dedicated to my wife,
Lt. Colonel Esther M. Satterlee.
We knew it would be a joy
but we had no idea
it would be so interesting.

CONTENTS

FOREWORD

From the pen of Lt. Colonel Allen Satterlee comes
the latest of four *Revealed* Bible studies (*Joy Revealed*
[Philippians]; *The Kingdom Revealed* [The Sermon
On The Mount]; *Pilgrimage Revealed* [First Peter]).
*Heavenly Places Revealed: A Thirty-one Day Devo-
tional Guide to Ephesians* is lifted from the pages of
Paul's letter to the church in Ephesus, admonishing and
encouraging Christians there on themes of the nature
of election, the new family of God, and how Christians
ought to love.

Satterlee's intent is to provide a thirty-one-day devo-
tional exploration; but the month-long lineup could just
as easily be spread over several months as a midweek
Bible study. His illustrations are down to earth and
connect with readers of all ages. An example comes

from a throwback to the television comedy classic, *The Beverly Hillbillies*, which offers the premise that all of us have a little Jed Clampett in us—ignorant of the fact that as children of the King we have unlimited inherited riches.

The book is expository in nature, beginning even with Paul's customary introduction of his letter to his flock, and ending with personal salutations. Each chapter ends with a handful of discussion questions, ideal for personal introspection and/or group discussion.

Only three topics are expanded to two chapters each—"Power Through His Spirit," "God's View Of Marriage," and "Spiritual Warfare." Those three topics alone are of immense interest and even controversy among the Body of Christ in these modern times.

One common question is pondered around the globe: What is Heaven like? *Heavenly Places Revealed*, through Paul's interpretation of a believer's interaction with God and one another, comes as close as anything on this side of Glory.

—Major Frank Duracher

INTRODUCTION

The letter to the Ephesians contains one of the most complete expositions of the Christian faith, not only as it is lived from day to day, but against the backdrop of spiritual realities beyond this realm. For example, we see spiritual warfare not only waged in the present moment with the enemy at hand, but Paul tells us that our struggle is part of a battle "against the powers of this dark world and against the spiritual forces of evil in the heavenly realms" (Ephesians 6:12). Like a great camera lens, Paul takes us from a panoramic view on the one hand and an up-close view in the next.

Few books of the Bible are more quoted or referred to than Ephesians. As we take a look closer, we will find that Paul's skillful wording has shades of meaning that make it even richer than a cursory read.

Major themes of the book include the mystery of God, who created, from Jewish and Gentile believers, the new people of God. Paul frequently uses the phrase "in Christ" to characterize the believer's life.

The letter is not without controversy. Although it comes to us as a letter to the Ephesian church, there are no references to any people in Ephesus, even though Paul labored there for three years.[1] The prevailing theory is that rather than a specific letter to Ephesus, this was a more general letter to the churches in Asia Minor (modern day Turkey), with the Ephesian copy of the letter coming to us.[2]

Having said that, Ephesus was the primary city in this area with a population of more than 300,000. A major port, it was also home to the Temple of Artemis, or Diana, as the goddess was known. Supposedly brought to earth by Zeus, it contained a statue of the goddess housed in a magnificent structure that was one of the Seven Wonders of the Ancient World. Pilgrims to the temple added to the crowds in this important seaport city. As time went by, the sea retreated, leaving the city abandoned.[3] As a result, some of the most magnificent intact ruins are found in the ancient city of Ephesus.

Because of the importance of Ephesus and the

relevance of the content to the early church in its environs, this book treats it as the primary locale.

Ephesians is considered by most scholars to have been written during one of Paul's imprisonments, probably around 59–61 AD.[4] The audience is primarily Gentile.

Although Ephesians can be read through by most people in less than an hour, this book breaks it into thirty-one sections. We encourage you to slow down and prayerfully consider what the Holy Spirit says to you through its magnificent teachings so that you can be all you were meant to be "in Christ."

PAUL, AN APOSTLE

EPHESIANS 1:1-2

*"Paul, an apostle of Christ Jesus by
the will of God, to God's holy people in
Ephesus, the faithful in Christ Jesus:
Grace and peace to you from God our
Father and the Lord Jesus Christ."*

Who Am I?

How a person introduces himself or herself de-
pends on the circumstances. If in an official capacity or where authority needs to be established,
a title might be used such as professor, doctor, or
captain. If meeting a person on a date, it is usually
simply by a first name. If in a social situation where

the people are unfamiliar, first and last names are in order. The introduction is the first step toward an outcome, whether that be establishing or deepening a relationship, or assuming a task. I confess to times of being uncertain how to introduce myself, particularly when I am confused about the expectations of a social setting. When crossing cultures, this can be even more confusing.

Paul, an Apostle

Paul wasted no time in introducing himself by the only credentials that count, "an apostle of Christ Jesus by the will of God." Although the Greek root for apostle means "sent one," here it is likely used by Paul to establish his authority in an official office he held along with the original Twelve. In his capacity he wrote this letter to a cluster of churches rather than a specific one (see Introduction).

Far more important than his office was that he was where he was, writing to them in this moment, with all that follows because he was there by the will of God. This is not some wistful claim but one rooted in certainty, in authority. When one is certain that she is in the will of God there is no need to approach any given task with an apology or sheepishly, but rather assertively.

The will of God is not only where we are rooted as believers in our actions. It is what will prevail over all of creation when our Lord establishes His rule once and for all on earth and by extension, over all of creation. If you are in the will of God, you can say confidently that you are a sent one, armed for the battle with every confidence that God is with you.

God's Holy People
Paul addressed this letter to God's holy people, the ones set aside for His purpose and His glory. This holiness is not the result of something we as His people have grasped but what He has freely bestowed upon the hearts fully abandoned to Him. Though you might blush to make that claim, to fail to testify to God's sanctifying power and presence in you is to deny Him and His power. Jesus came among us not only to provide the means for our forgiveness and to allow us to be born again but so sin would no longer mark our days or define our lives.

Holiness not only speaks of the quality of our experience but our position. We have been set apart, the literal meaning of the word "sanctify." Not set apart from people so that we live over and above them, not deigning to stoop down to their level. Instead, we have made our hearts His offering, and live our lives for His glory. We have been set aside for Him and so we set aside everything that stands in the way of Him, having His complete way within our lives.

Are you holy?

Faithful in Christ Jesus

Paul then addressed them as the "faithful in Christ Jesus." Faithful in what?

First, they were faithful in their witness. In these days, there were no casual believers, no nominal Christians. To take a stand for Christ was to risk everything. For some it meant death. For others it meant the loss of property and livelihoods. For still others, it meant the scorn and daily indignities that come with being universally despised. As it still is in some parts of the world, to claim Christ meant that a believer was disowned from her family, dead to them. Yet, these believers were faithful in their witness so much so that the truth of their lives laid bare the emptiness of those without Christ.

Second, they were faithful in their beliefs. These letters of Paul were not just initiated by him. The early church was hungry to know the full particulars of their doctrines. They had the Old Testament, and this was a solid grounding, but Christ's coming had opened up new understanding, new experiences, and the implications were enormous. It affected what people ate, how they conducted their social lives, how their relationships and family lives were structured, how they worked and worshipped. For the Jews who had been converted, it was a reboot of their understanding. For the Gentile believers, it was a whole new world that shook every concept upon which they had formed their lives. They wanted to know the how, the what, the where, and the who. When Paul and the other apostles taught, believers wanted not to only learn something new but to faithfully put into practice what was being taught.

Thirdly, they were faithful in their love for the Lord. It was not only when they worshipped with other believers or sought to evangelize, but they sought the Lord in their quiet moments, in the tiny choices where the reality of what they professed was tested in choosing what their Lord wanted over what might have been otherwise acceptable. He was not only Lord over the mighty moments of triumph but over the little opportunities for obedience. Here love was proven in a fleeting whispered prayer, in a truth that sacrificed an advantage to stand firm, in a gentle answer when an angry one first came to mind.

DISCUSSION QUESTIONS

1) How is the present day similar to first century Christianity? How is it different?

2) How does it feel to say, "I am holy"? If it is uncomfortable, why is that? If you can do so confidently, upon what is that based?

3) How do you define faithfulness to God?

2
ADOPTED

EPHESIANS 1:3-5

"Praise be to the God and Father of our Lord Jesus Christ, who has blessed us in the heavenly realms with every spiritual blessing in Christ. For he chose us in him before the creation of the world to be holy and blameless in his sight. In love he predestined us for adoption to sonship through Jesus Christ, in accordance with his pleasure and will—"

Adopted

There are few subjects dearer to my heart than adoption. Before I was born, my mother surrendered a child for adoption who, after more than seventy years, I only recently met. Later, my brothers and I were adopted by our then stepfather when my mother remarried. And still later, my wife and I adopted four children. And finally, because of some family situations, a generation later we adopted five of our grandchildren. As significant as these are, they are but a shadow of what our adoption is as children of God.

After his brief introduction, Paul immediately launched into praise for what God through Christ has done for believers.

God Has Blessed Us

Not with random blessings here and there but with *every* blessing. The Church Father Jerome remarked on this passage, "Spiritual blessings are in the heavens because earth is too small to circumscribe a spiritual blessing."[5] It is not only the immensity of our blessing in Christ that is so notable, but also the certainty that the continuance of our blessing would wear out every clock that ever kept time. Our blessings can only be calculated by eternity. The blessing of our salvation is meant to carry us through, past the last beating of our hearts and the final breath in our lungs.

It is a mistake to think that these blessings are all material or that they will result in a change of status in this life. By receiving Christ, no poor man suddenly moved into a mansion nor did a slave suddenly find she was granted her freedom. It is just as much a mistake to think that people now living for the Lord have punched their tickets for an easy ride the rest of their lives through. We are not necessarily blessed with the paltry stuff of this life but rather with what cannot perish or waste away.

A Destiny for Us

Each person has a destiny that God intends for him or her. Those of the Calvinist camp see this as God foreordaining who will be saved and who will be lost; that His grace, while expansive enough for the whole world, is only meant for a select few. But the Bible indicates over and over that the salvation of God, and what that means in how we develop and grow, is freely accessed because the bloodied hands of Christ reach out to the whosoever. True, not everyone receives it and so they deny themselves their God-given destiny. But it is there, nonetheless.

When Paul said, "He chose us," he was not necessarily saying God chose us as individuals to be saved or lost, but He chose us as a race. As much as we might love our dog or cat, animals have not been chosen for an eternal destiny nor to develop a spiritual life of communion with and service to God. As much as God might enjoy the praises of the angels, Christ did not die to save the angels that fell. God through Christ brought the possibility of salvation solely for the human race. With our gift of free will, we kneel before Him, seeking Him and His forgiveness in that grand act of salvation that grants us access into His life and plan.

God Adopts Us
Harold W. Hoehner helps us understand how this concept would have been understood by the first-century Christians:

"In the Roman law the procedure of adoption had two steps. In the first step, the son had to be released from the control of the natural father. This was done by a procedure whereby the father sold him as a slave three times to the adopter. The adopter would release him two times and he would automatically again come under his father's control. With the third sale, the adoptee was freed from his natural father. Regarding the second step, since the natural father no longer had any authority over him, the adopter became the new father with absolute control over him,

22

and he retained this control until the adoptee dies or the adopter frees him. The son was not responsible to his natural father but only to his newly acquired father. The purpose of the adoption was so that the adoptee could take the position of a natural son in order to continue the family line and maintain property owner-ship. This son became *patria potestas* in the next generation."[6]

The Church Father Chrysostom summarized the difference by saying it was like taking a poor, old, ill-clad, and famished leper and turning him into a rich, healthy, well attired, and satisfied youth.[7]

The old song says,

"I once was an outcast stranger on earth,
A sinner by choice, and an alien by birth,
But I've been adopted, my name's written down,
An heir to a mansion, a robe and a crown.

I'm the child of a king;
I'm the child of a king;
With Jesus, my Savior,
I'm the child of a king!"

–Harriett Eugenia Peck Buell
The Song Book of The Salvation Army
#877, vs. 3, chorus

DISCUSSION QUESTIONS

1) What is God's chosen destiny for you? How might things change if you fail to live for Him? How might they turn out if you stay within His will?

2) Imagine the worst person you know and then imagine that person serving Christ. What does that say about what God intends for each individual?

3) How does the picture of adoption define your relationship with God?

3

LAVISHED ON US

EPHESIANS 1:6-10

"To the praise of his glorious grace, which he has freely given us in the one he loves. In him we have redemption through his blood, the forgiveness of sins, in accordance with the riches of God's grace that he lavished on us. With all wisdom and understanding, he made known to us the mystery of his will according to his good pleasure, which he purposed in Christ, to be put into effect when the times reach their fulfillment—to bring unity to all things in heaven and on earth under Christ."

Riches

In west Texas there is an oil field called Yates Pool. Originally a sheep ranch, Mr. Yates couldn't scratch out enough of a living to avoid being on government assistance. One day, a crew from an oil company asked if they could drill a well. He agreed. At 1,115 feet, they hit a huge reserve that had the potential of producing 125,000 barrels of oil a day. While Yates was on welfare, he was really a multi-millionaire. He simply didn't know it.[8]

Paul did not want the Ephesians to be unaware of the riches that they had in Christ. He declares that what they have "He has freely given us in the One He loves." When our heart bows to Him and receives the gift of salvation, we are only scratching the surface of what is our legacy in Him. It is not held by some trustee that begrudges us access to what is ours but given to us freely. We are rich beyond measure, which makes the spiritual poverty of so many believers that much more tragic. What do we have?

Redemption Through His Blood

Paul was familiar with the Jewish religious tradition of sacrifices and offerings. When one sacrifice or offering was given, another one was due for something else. In front of the Temple in Jerusalem, a line snaked through the streets composed of those offering their lambs, cows, goats, and birds. The blood trickled endlessly down from an altar that was never satisfied. The worshippers would have to come back and do it again. For those who had worshipped other gods it was even worse. It wasn't one god who demanded satisfaction but scores of them, each with his or her own specialty that the worshipper had to satisfy.

Here we stand in grace where we have redemption, not through some little innocent animal, but through the Son of God Himself. Only a small number of people actually saw His blood flow on that Good Friday, but all the world can experience its cleansing. We need not see it to have it work in our hearts.

The forgiveness of sins does not come as a trickle, forcing us to lap our tongues on the drops of grace that dribble out. No—it is lavish. Not drops but a waterfall; not pennies but a king's ransom; not a croaking whisper but a great symphony. In our walk with the Lord, we are not forced to go to God and beg Him for a morsel. He has a feast before us with our dishes refilled before we can eat what's there.

All Wisdom and Understanding

Wisdom is the application of knowledge while understanding is grasping the fundamentals. These gifts are in place so that we not only experience what God is doing in us, but also consider what is happening within us and what our place is in the plan of God. Humans possess the unique ability to think about thinking, unknown in the animal kingdom. We can, in a sense, stand outside of ourselves and consider what is going on within us. God impacts us with that gift as we stand in wonder of His work in our lives.

Then there is His guidance so we can choose what is right, discern what comes to us by seeing and hearing with the mind of Christ. The Holy Spirit is our teacher and director so that we can move forward with confidence.

The Mystery of His Will

The Jewish people had a distinct advantage over the rest of humanity in that centuries earlier, God had brought them close so they could see and understand what He was doing in the world. But even they could not perceive what the full expanse of His will was. He worked through the Jewish people, but if things had gone as they ought, they would have become the conduit as God reached out for the redemption of the whole world. Instead, they largely held it tight to their chests, glorying in their favored place.

The mystery revealed, and one which Paul constantly marveled at, was that salvation was for every child of Adam's race. The Gentiles were not just welcome but sought after to join the family of God. Nor would it be that there would be different branches in this family. Instead, there would be but one family, one new people of God. The schism that had been the source of so much hatred and envy and warfare was healed by the scarred hands of Christ.

But there is more to this. Paul says that it was to "bring unity to all things in heaven and on earth under Christ." The schism between Jews and Gentiles was great, but the divide between heaven and earth was greater. We recall that in the Garden of Eden God walked there to commune with our first parents. The way between heaven and earth was open, but when the Fall happened the door slammed shut. God would not have sin in His heaven, so humankind was barred access.

But in Christ, that barrier has been broken down. The angels likely were amazed that God maintained interest in the tainted creation, the pathetic creatures that groveled through generations, seeming to learn nothing along the way. Those same angels likely felt their hearts break as they watched the Son of God cruelly treated, betrayed, abandoned, and then tortured until His last breath left Him.

But now, to find that the humanity that had been such a disappointment was unified with heaven again! What wonder! Who but God could show such lavish love? Who but God could conceive of such a story? Who but God could unify that which had been so far removed?

DISCUSSION QUESTIONS

1) How had the sacrificial system showed both separation from God and His desire to have communion with people?

2) Think about how God has worked in your life. What has surprised you? What do you think He is doing with you now?

3) Why is God's unifying work described as a mystery?

4

SEALED BY THE SPIRIT

EPHESIANS 1:11-14

"In him we were also chosen, having been predestined according to the plan of him who works out everything in conformity with the purpose of his will, in order that we, who were the first to put our hope in Christ, might be for the praise of his glory. And you also were included in Christ when you heard the message of truth, the gospel of your salvation. When you believed, you were marked in him with a seal, the promised Holy Spirit, who is a deposit guaranteeing our inheritance until the redemption of those who are God's possession—to the praise of his glory."

Election

One of the most difficult concepts in Christianity is what is called "election." A key passage to our understanding of it is this one. As we discussed earlier, those of the Calvinist tradition assert that God has from all eternity chosen those who will be saved and those who will be lost. This has been done, not based on the merits of an individual but on grace alone. They would say that because of the depraved nature of individuals, it is a wonder that God would choose *anyone at all* since no one deserves salvation. And since God has chosen individuals for salvation, that salvation cannot be lost in that God has sovereignly ruled who is to be saved. No act, then, can merit salvation nor can any act disqualify someone from salvation.

Others see election as working quite differently. The Bible clearly speaks of election in multiple places, beginning with God selecting the nation of Israel as His chosen people. A sample reference is Deuteronomy 7:6: "For you are a people holy to the LORD your God. The LORD your God has chosen you out of all the peoples on the face of the earth to be His people, His treasured possession." Part of their election was to receive the Promised Land, the gift of the Holy Scriptures, the legacy of the Law, and the Temple (Tabernacle). They did nothing to earn this as God showed His favor to them.

Individual Response to Covenant

But with that election as a people, there was still the matter of how individuals responded to their favored status. We have those who appreciated the grace they enjoyed, such as Joseph, Moses, Samuel, David, Isaiah, Elijah, and many others. But there were also those who despised their birthright, turning away from the love that God showed them to live lives of rebellion. We can quickly name Saul, Jeroboam, Ahab, and Manasseh as well as those who started well but later turned their backs on God, the most startling example being Solomon. Although among the elect of Israel, God's chosen people, they still had the capacity to live in a way totally foreign to the covenant that God had established. To make things even more interesting, there were non-Jews who became believers and in doing so, except for legitimate ownership of a piece of the Promised Land, enjoyed the benefits that the elect of Israel claimed.

When Jesus came as a Jew, He perfectly fulfilled the human side of the God's covenant that had been extended to the Hebrew people. His perfect obedience was unrivaled not only in His generation but in the history of humanity. Because of His divine nature, He also understood, as no one before had, the intention of God's election. The nation of Israel was meant to be the gateway people to all the people of the earth, communicating God's salvation for all. When God established His promise through Abraham, He said, "I will multiply your descendants as the stars of heaven and will give your descendants all these lands; and by your descendants *all the nations of the earth shall be blessed*" (Genesis 26:4, italics added).

Then Came the Gentiles

Soon after the Church was launched, God declared unmistakably that Gentiles were included. In Acts 10, Peter had a vision that resulted in action with the household of Cornelius whereby the floodgates of salvation opened to all peoples. Here in Ephesians, Paul explained more about the theological framework that made it clear that while Israel as God's covenant people has not been pushed aside, the blessings that were hers as a people are now opened to all. The exception is the Promised Land since this was a once and for all transaction of God. The sole condition to this election is coming to God through Christ.

Election then, is still a matter of grace alone. None of us has ever done one thing in any way that we could present to God and with it, show Him that we merit His salvation. We have a host of sins that more soundly condemn us than righteous acts that commend us. When you ask Christ into your heart, His Holy Spirit cleanses what could otherwise never be clean because of the merits of Christ's blood. You have abandoned your citizenship from a country at war with God to become a citizen of His country with all the rights and privileges therein.

If you struggle to grasp this, you have joined the generations who, while they rejoice in what God has done, are dumbfounded by the breadth of all it entails. As Paul has said in this passage, we are "God's possession—to the praise of His glory" (Ephesians 1:14).

DISCUSSION QUESTIONS

1) What did election mean for the nation of Israel? What did it not mean?

2) How does a person become one of God's elect?

3) How do election and grace work together?

5

EYES OF YOUR HEART

EPHESIANS 1:15-23

*"For this reason, ever since I heard about
your faith in the Lord Jesus and your love for
all God's people, I have not stopped giving
thanks for you, remembering you in my prayers.
I keep asking that the God of our Lord Jesus
Christ, the glorious Father, may give you the
Spirit of wisdom and revelation, so that you
may know him better. I pray that the eyes of
your heart may be enlightened in order that
you may know the hope to which he has called
you, the riches of his glorious inheritance in
his holy people, and his incomparably great
power for us who believe. That power is the
same as the mighty strength he exerted when*

he raised Christ from the dead and seated
him at his right hand in the heavenly realms,
far above all rule and authority, power and
dominion, and every name that is invoked, not
only in the present age but also in the one to
come. And God placed all things under his feet
and appointed him to be head over everything
for the church, which is his body, the fullness
of him who fills everything in every way."

Clearer Vision

Not too long ago my doctor said it was time to
have two cataracts removed. They had been slowly
forming for a few years and now had reached the
point where they were definitely interfering with
my sight. I followed the preferred procedure, which
is to remove the cataract from one eye and then a
week later from the other. I was amazed to see the
difference. Several times I closed the eye with the
cataract, then opened it. In my right eye, everything was clear but in my left eye there was a dingy
yellow tint on everything. The change had come so
gradually over the years that I did not realize how
my vision had been affected. But now, I was able to
see clearly again.

In addressing the young church in Ephesus, Paul prayed that "the eyes of your heart may be enlightened." It wasn't until the gospel gave them sight that they could begin to realize how blind they had become. And when sight came, they saw things beyond anything they could have imagined.

Seeing What Was Unseen

They saw hope, not some wishy-washy wistful sentiment that is born of fairy tales. Rather, when the Bible speaks of hope it means solid certainty that something is coming; it will happen as surely as the sun will declare the arrival of a new day. As Merida has said, "Our salvation is marked by massive hope."[9]

They found power. Paul made it clear. This is "incomparably great power." It is the power that finds that even if He whispers, galaxies must obediently form from nothing. It is the power that made weightless dust become bone and sinew as it rose to become someone who was in the image of God. It was the power that shone when an Egyptian ruler who fancied himself a god met the fugitive shepherd named Moses. He would bow after being crushed, his nation blasted into submission. It is the power that left an Assyrian army gathered at the gates of Jerusalem, trying to gather what survivors it could as it limped back home. But most remarkably, it was the power that stood when Satan thought he had finally won. Instead, he found himself plowed aside by a resurrected Savior. Had Satan gathered all his demonic forces outside the tomb and used their combined strength to push against the stone— and in many ways that is exactly what he attempted—he would have found the stone slingshotted into irrelevance as the mighty Son of God reasserted His claim on the earth He created.

Heavenly Realms

So complete was this victory that no corner of the vast universe, no place in the world of spirits or angels was off limits to His rule. Nor could even the epochs of time pass or the unfolding of future ages find a moment that He did not occupy and control. How did Paul say it? God "seated Him as His right hand in the heavenly realms, far above all rule and authority, power and dominion, and every name that invoked, not only in the present age but also in the one to come. And God placed all things under his feet and appointed him head over everything" (1:21–22). In saying that God placed all things under His feet, Paul employed an expression that was used of the winner of a duel, who underscores his dominance by placing his foot on the neck of his fallen enemy after throwing him to the ground.[10]

More than proclaiming Christ's absolute power and victory, Paul told us that for we who are His followers, there is a very important reason that touches us in it. It is "for the church" (1:23). We are His Body, an image repeated elsewhere in the New Testament. Hoehner remarks, "One good reason to use the human body as an analogy is that it conveys the idea of an organic unity that is animated by the head ... The members of the body of Christ are bound to each other and are related to Christ as our Redeemer, sustainer and head."[11]

And this Church, so despised and ridiculed, attacked and undermined, is "the fullness of Him who fills everything in every way' (1:23). Look around, people. The Church is the fullness of Christ. It should encourage us, humble us, frighten us, and challenge us. God's purpose in this world will be done through His Church, the Body of believers who have found their life in Him. There is no other plan. Because as far as God is concerned, there is no better plan.

DISCUSSION QUESTIONS

1) How would you describe Christian hope to an unbeliever?

2) The author has written about some ways that God has displayed His power. What other ways can you think of?

3) In what ways does the Church function as the Body of Christ?

6

DEAD IN SIN

EPHESIANS 2:1-3

"As for you, you were dead in your transgressions and sins, in which you used to live when you followed the ways of this world and of the ruler of the kingdom of the air, the spirit who is now at work in those who are disobedient. All of us also lived among them at one time, gratifying the cravings of our flesh and following its desires and thoughts. Like the rest, we were by nature deserving of wrath."

Dead

What more descriptive metaphor for the sinful life could there be than "dead"? Did Paul mean we are lifeless like a rock that never lived at all? Dead, like some frozen asteroid tumbling in a meaningless orbit somewhere in space? Things like that are not only lifeless but incapable of ever having life. We might paint a face on a stone, take a hunk of marble and chisel it into a statue that in every way mimics the dimensions and shapes of a human body, or grind dust into a compound and pour it into a mold to be shaped like a living thing. But dead it would remain. Lifeless. We can't even say it's hopeless because no life could be trafficked through it. Is that what Paul meant?

Or did he mean that we were as good as dead? That we were diseased from head to toe, filled with putrefying sores, wracked with unending pain, and waiting out the time until the last breath is drawn? Are we not more like the comatose patient in intensive care who lies motionless, aided by machines to breathe and to function at the basest level? This one cannot affect his own cure, cannot get up to go get the life-saving treatment even if it was just across the room. No, this man must be given help from someone outside who administers it on behalf of one so helpless. He is a dead man in every respect, except that somehow a whisp of life remains. This is more of what Paul means.

The Diagnosis

When the Holy Spirit begins His work in our life, He must help us see our own need. If we keep with the patient analogy, the one suffering must be roused to consciousness from his deadly stupor to be able to recognize the dire situation in which he exists.

Or perhaps a better way to see this is as a situation that too often tragically happens. Here is a woman who goes to the doctor for some minor pain or for a checkup, only to receive a diagnosis of an inoperable health condition that leaves her with only days, weeks, or months to live.

That is the exact situation all people are in before they receive Christ as Savior. We live our lives unaware that within us we are carrying our own doom. We might feel fine or maybe a bit annoyed. Perhaps we are downright miserable but not enough to seek a change. Meanwhile every day pushes us closer to the edge of eternity. But the Holy Spirit shines His light where never a light shone, and our true condition is revealed. We are dead in our trespasses and sins.

Trespasses and Sins

Although it sounds like Paul is repeating himself by saying "trespasses and sins," in fact, they have different meanings. Sin in Greek is the word *harm-*

artia, which literally means "missing the mark." It is a term from archery, with the idea that the archer shoots his arrow, but it falls short of the target. Spiritually, it is to fail to do what should be done, a partial obedience, a shying away from full submission. Rather than taking up the cross and following Christ, it is looking at the cross and turning away, judging that the weight is too much of a sacrifice.

The second word that is translated as transgression is the Greek word *paraptōma*, which literally means to "slip or fall, losing the way or straying."[12] This is more intentional sin. Here is not a failure to do what is right, but a deliberate decision to do what is wrong. It can be heard in statements such as, "I don't care what _____, I'll do as I please." Spiritually, it is to know I am not to lie, yet I lie anyway. It is to know that sexual sin is an affront to God and as Paul says elsewhere, "whoever sins sexually, sins against their own body" (1 Corinthians 6:18). In this, then, a transgression is more serious because it is a purposeful act of rebellion.

Enslaved by "Freedom"

Paul reminds the Ephesians that this state of death, this hopelessness created not only by their nature but their choices, is where they used to live.

In the illusion of what they thought was "freedom," they were instead slaves to the "ruler of the kingdom of the air." Satan held the reins, bridling them with insatiable appetites and unrelenting shame.

Nor was it only the Ephesians. Paul switches from "you" in the second verse to "us." None of us escaped, no matter how reputable we passed ourselves off to be. What person doesn't have a moment or an action or a thought that if brought out into the open would be devastating? Like the crowd gathered around the woman caught in adultery, we *know* we cannot cast a stone based on the credentials of our innocence. It is not only you. It is us. All of us.

If God were to judge then destroy each one of us, none could point to our own purity and claim we were not deserving. The wrath of God is our destiny, the correct sentence of God's court of law. The Church Father Tertullian correctly remarked, "We create the grounds for the Creator's wrath ourselves."[13] Not my parents, my spouse, my children, society, my enemies, or my friends. This crime is laid personally at our feet with our fingerprints and DNA all over it. "Guilty!" is the ringing verdict of our unregenerate life.

DISCUSSION QUESTIONS

1) Which picture of being dead seems to you more accurate? Stone dead or terminally diseased with no hope of a cure?

2) How have you seen sin and transgression at work in your life?

3) Why do you think Paul felt it necessary to help the Ephesians understand the depth of their depravity?

7

ALIVE IN CHRIST

EPHESIANS 2:4-10

"But because of his great love for us, God, who is rich in mercy, made us alive with Christ even when we were dead in transgressions—it is by grace you have been saved. And God raised us up with Christ and seated us with him in the heavenly realms in Christ Jesus, in order that in the coming ages he might show the incomparable riches of his grace, expressed in his kindness to us in Christ Jesus. For it is by grace you have been saved, through faith—and this is not from yourselves, it is the gift of God—not by works, so that no one can boast. For we are God's handiwork, created in Christ Jesus to do good works, which God prepared in advance for us to do."

But Because

The shadows of despair outlined in the first three verses of this chapter are blasted away by the bright light that starts, "But because ..." We were on the gallows, the noose around our necks, all appeals exhausted because our guilt was beyond question, the gravity of our crime demanding justice.

Enter God's love, the very love that we callously pushed away. As William Barclay points out, "Sin is a crime, not against law, but against love."[14] Nonetheless, in the gift of salvation, God's love takes the noose from around our necks, loosens the shackles, and leads us gently away from our fate. Mercy is the operative word for His intercession, "even when were dead in transgressions." The stench of our decay is swallowed by the sweet aroma of God's mercy.

Sentence Passed to Another

Our execution has been stayed. For anyone who is sure he is taking his last breaths that is a great enough display of love and mercy. But there is so much more! The Lord Jesus Christ's own execution was not stopped as He felt His human life ebb slowly away. Although His torn and abused body was hidden away in a cold tomb, He has pushed aside the worst that Satan could do in the victorious moment of resurrection. God raised Him and exalted Him and look! "God raised *us up* with Him!" He has been seated in heaven and "seated us up with him in the heavenly realms."

Get this. We were damned criminals, totally diseased living dead, all hope extinguished to do even the smallest thing on our own behalf. But God changed all that, not only wiping our record clean, stopping our punishment, but giving us a place in the very heavens with the Savior who rescued us. Sit back and think about that. These are the "incomparable riches of his grace, expressed to us in his kindness to us in Christ Jesus."

Grace Through Faith

"For it is by grace you have been saved, through faith—and this is not from yourselves, it is the gift of God— not by works, so that no one can boast" (2:8–9). Paul helped us with one of the best sentences ever to understand salvation. He spoke of grace, which has classically been defined as "the unmerited favor of God." But how can we understand better what that means?

Here is a newborn baby. She had nothing to do with her formation in the mother's womb. When it came time to be born, she could do nothing to aid in that process. In the birth process, there are those around to assist with her entry into the world. With her first breath in an alien environment, arms lovingly wrap her, and tender voices soothe her. She cannot feed herself, talk, walk, or even return the smiles so lovingly directed her way. She is loved simply for being. There is nothing, absolutely nothing, she can do to provide for herself. She is living in grace, the unmerited favor of those who love her and provide for her. As infants in Christ, we are regarded by God with an infinitely greater grace than any of us can possibly show to a newborn.

As she grows, though still living in grace, she is expected to do more. When she can, she will hold her head up, roll over, and return smiles. As she matures, she will learn and be given more responsibility. This does not make her any more loved than when she was a newborn infant, but it is reasonable to expect that she builds on her abilities and does something with them. Indeed, a healthy individual wants to do more. That is works at work.

God's Handiwork

Finally, Paul says we are God's handiwork. Original sin marred us at the beginning, but our choices made a bad situation even worse. Then grace entered and not only saved us from sin's awful penalty, but God began to make us into something better than we ever might have been otherwise.

Here is a giant slab of marble, wrestled from the earth. It is cleaned off and scrubbed, removing everything that is not marble. Then comes the sculptor. With his skill he takes off huge chunks here. Then with a chisel and other tools, he begins to do finer work. In time we forget that this was a piece of ugly, shapeless stone because of the work of art that is now a statue. That is what God does with us. We were ugly and formless but with His great skill, He makes us into something beautiful, fit for His own purposes.

DISCUSSION QUESTIONS

1) What does it mean to you when Paul says, "God raised us up with Christ"?

2) How does the illustration of a newborn help us understand grace?

3) How is God forming you to be His handiwork?

8

BROUGHT NEAR

EPHESIANS 2:11-13

*"Therefore, remember that formerly you
who are Gentiles by birth and called
"uncircumcised" by those who call themselves
"the circumcision" (which is done in the body
by human hands)—remember that at that
time you were separate from Christ, excluded
from citizenship in Israel and foreigners to
the covenants of the promise, without hope
and without God in the world. But now in
Christ Jesus you who once were far away have
been brought near by the blood of Christ."*

The Blight of Segregated Separation

As a Southerner who has lived a little while, I have memories of the days of segregation. I was quite young when I first realized there were other people in my town who looked different than me. They were over there, and I was over here. It did not occur to me that there was anything more to it. Only later did I discover that this was legislated, that somehow people on my side of things thought that things would go awry if the two races mixed. When I became aware of what was happening, my young sense of justice was angered by this. When the civil rights movement began to gather momentum, I was in favor of it. Eventually, laws changed and segregation lost its legal footing. But saying it was over and making it so was quite another thing. While we have come light years since then, there are those reminders that some continue to think they are born in a place of higher favor that dictates they distance and dislike those who are not the same as "us."

Not Like Us

When Christianity began to spread beyond the bounds of Jerusalem and the cradle of Judaism, the inbred prejudice of not only the Jews, but other races became a hurdle to the gospel spreading as Christ intended. No doubt the first Christians assumed that because they were all Jewish, and Jesus had been Jewish, and they were aware of their status as God's chosen people, any believers outside of Judaism would become Jews once they accepted Christ. After all, their standards stated that it was unlawful to help a Gentile mother in childbirth because it would result in another Gentile being brought into the world.[15] The Jewish people were in for the rudest of surprises.

In Acts 10, a dramatic revelation is coming to Peter. From that time forward, the Church understood, as it had never had before, that salvation was for the whole world. When later Paul was converted, the self-described "Hebrew of the Hebrews," whose own jealousy for the Jewish faith led to murderous rampages, found that of all people he was to be the apostle to the Gentiles. There could hardly have been a more ironic twist than this. But as Paul was led by the Spirit, he realized that the new believers were not to be another iteration of the Jewish faith, but that God was forming a new people, the Body of Christ, the Church.

One of the first Church councils was held to confirm that the Gentiles need not submit to all the Jewish laws and ceremonies (Acts 16). It was

agreed that while the new believers were obligated
to honor the moral law, they need not observe the
ceremonial or civil law as outlined in the Old Testament. The curious exception was eating meat with
blood still in it. That would seem to have settled it
but just like the decision to dismantle desegregation
in the Southern United States took a while and a lot
of pain to work out, the same thing happened in the
Church. As a result, we find that Paul in several of
his letters keeps circling back to this issue. It wasn't
a doctrinal fine point but vital to have this understanding embraced and practiced.

Paul uses a derogatory term that the Jews used,
accurate as it may have been, to describe the Gentiles: uncircumcised. This rite alone was a clear
mark of separation that distinguished them from a
world the Jewish people felt was untouchable. Paul
noted that the Gentiles before becoming believers
were "separate from Christ, excluded from citizenship in Israel and foreigners to the covenants
of promise, without hope, and without God in the
world" (v 12).

Brought Near

"But now" leapt from Paul's quill and the scroll
as he wrote. "You who once were far away have

been brought near by the blood of Christ" (v 13). The borders that were closed to you, the doors that had been slammed on your fingers, the shunning that greeted you in the streets are in the past tense. It's not that the Gentiles had suddenly become Jews, but they were "being included along with the Jew *in Christ Jesus* (italics in the original)."[16]

When integration was forced by the courts, Willie Clarke, who sat next to me in high school band, became a friend. One day, for some reason, he asked me to take him by his home. He invited me in, the first time I had stepped foot in an African American person's home. As he got what he needed, I was left alone in his living room where I carefully looked around at the picture of Christ and the portrait of Martin Luther King, Jr. I felt unworthy to be there, knowing the history between the races. Upon reflection, I realized that segregation had not only denied black people a place, but it had also denied white people access. Willie is a brother in Christ, making this memory that much more cherished.

When the Holy Spirit melted away the differences between the Jews and the Gentiles to form the new people of God, both sides found what they missed as well as discovered what they now had together in Christ.

DISCUSSION QUESTIONS

1) Does the parallel between segregation in the United States serve as a way of understanding the separation between the Jews and the Gentiles? Why or why not?

2) What does it mean to you to know that through Christ you have been "brought near" to all that was denied to you before you were saved?

3) How difficult is it to set aside prejudices that have been taught through the generations?

9

JESUS, OUR PEACE

EPHESIANS 2:14-18

"For he himself is our peace, who has made the two groups one and has destroyed the barrier, the dividing wall of hostility, by setting aside in his flesh the law with its commands and regulations. His purpose was to create in himself one new humanity out of the two, thus making peace, and in one body to reconcile both of them to God through the cross, by which he put to death their hostility. He came and preached peace to you who were far away and peace to those who were near. For through him we both have access to the Father by one Spirit."

Peace Child

In 1962, Don and Carol Richardson sought to reach the Sawi people for Christ, a cannibalistic tribe on the island of New Guinea. Although the first white people to ever visit them, they were welcomed enthusiastically because the tribe had heard that missionaries brought medicine, steel axes, and nylon fishing nets. The tribe prided itself in its practice of making friends with someone, then when they were not expecting it, murdering and eating them. When the Sawis heard the gospel story of Christ's death, they cheered Judas because he exemplified that very ethic.

The Richardsons were making no headway and decided to give up. The Sawi were distressed because of losing the benefits that came with the missionaries. It was then that the couple stumbled on the only way the Sawi would honor a peace. "An exchange of infants between villages is a 'Tarop Tim,' or 'Peace Child.' As long as the Peace Child lives, peace is guaranteed. Although most any other murder is honorable, killing a Peace Child is a despicable act."[17] The Richardsons presented Jesus as God's Peace Child who, because He is eternal, guarantees peace forever. The message got through and the Sawi began to accept Christ as Savior.

Seeds of Animosity

As Paul further discussed how Jesus "has destroyed the barrier, the dividing wall of hostility between the Jews and Gentiles, he proclaimed that "Jesus is our peace" (v 14); that such hostility historically should be of little surprise.

The Jewish nation had struggled to exist almost from its birth. Enemies constantly flooded over its porous borders. Its geography placed in squarely in the path of warring empires to its north and south. When one nation wanted to invade another, Israel served as a highway. The armies may have been after bigger game than Israel but when they were going after each other, Israel's resources, treasures, manpower, and strategic position made it seem ripe for the picking. The Israelites were to be exploited, then tossed aside. Some, like the Greeks, were not happy with only using the Jewish people and wanted to integrate them into their culture, wiping away their religion and separate identity. Little wonder that after centuries of this, there was a seething resentment among the Jewish people toward the Gentiles.

But the Gentiles had their own reasons for resenting the Jews. When most religions met each other, they found a way to blend theirs with the religions that were new to them. When your pantheon of gods has a few hundred, what's wrong with adding a few dozen more? But the Jews would have none of this. Not only would they not blend their religion, but they ridiculed other religions, denied the reality of everyone else's gods while stubbornly declaring there was only one God—all others were pretenders. And while other religions had managed to accommodate prostitution and other depraved practices, the Jews insisted on a purity that was baffling to the Gentiles. Paradoxically, attracted to Judaism, he had to submit to surgery on his most private part. What an immodest requirement for a religion that defined modesty! It was as if the Jews wanted to keep to themselves, resenting rather than cooperating with any who had proven they could conquer and destroy them.

Breaking Barriers

Christianity introduced a new element. The millennia of resentment, hatred, misunderstanding, and mistrust was wiped away in Jesus. The Gentiles found His message as appealing as the Jews. In Christ there was a place to meet at a level and on a scale that never existed before. He was their peace. And in being their peace, it redefined everything for everyone. The Church Father Chrysostom, said, "It is as if one should melt down a statue of silver, and statue of lead, and the two come out gold."[18]

Here in the Body of Christ, the Church, there were no inborn advantages, no claims to a higher status because of race or nationality. There was an equality here that did not and could not exist without Christ. Culturally, differences remained as they do with the differences in gender, intelligence, athletic ability, genetics, talent, and a host of other qualities that mark us as individuals. But we have been united in one Father and each of us is a child of God, no more favored or less favored than the other. That is part of the peace that Jesus brings.

DISCUSSION QUESTIONS

1) How does the illustration of the Peace Child help you understand Jesus being our peace?

2) Given the historical hostility of the Jews and the Gentiles, how difficult or easy do you think it was for these two groups to embrace each other in the Church? Why?

3) How has Jesus been your peace?

10

FELLOW CITIZENS

EPHESIANS 2:19-22

*"Consequently, you are no longer foreigners
and strangers, but fellow citizens with God's
people and also members of his household,
built on the foundation of the apostles and
prophets, with Christ Jesus himself as the
chief cornerstone. In him the whole building
is joined together and rises to become a
holy temple in the Lord. And in him you
too are being built together to become a
dwelling in which God lives by his Spirit."*

Resident Foreigner

My wife and I had the privilege of serving over-seas in three different countries: Singapore, Papua New Guinea, and Jamaica. Although we were ap-pointed to these places by The Salvation Army, we still had to go through a process of being approved by each respective government to live and work there. A card was issued that we were to always have with us that stated that while we were not citizens of that country, we were there legally. The governments knew our citizenship was elsewhere and that in time, we would leave and go back home. We lived one place, but our eventual destination was somewhere else.

New People of God

After speaking about the reconciliation in Christ of the Jews and the Gentiles to form the new people of God, Paul moves on to speak about the signifi-cance of that. With respect to the kingdom of God, they were no longer "foreigners and strangers" (v 19). The two words, while similar, contained differ-ent ideas. The foreigner was someone like a tourist or someone just transiting through, like someone at an airport connecting to another flight. They were in and out, having no desire nor plan to stay more than a brief time. The stranger was quite different. As we were in the countries where we served, the stranger was someone who had come to stay for a while, perhaps years, but then move on. They had citizenship somewhere else.

As it happens now, some of those who only meant to be in a place temporarily decided they wanted to stay permanently. They sought to be citizens. Paul was saying that when we became part of the Church, the "members of his household," we were now granted permanent status as citizens with full rights to live and remain in this new place.

New Building

As Paul often did, he quickly changed to another metaphor, from citizenship to a building. This is no surprise. The Church was not only new in its existence, but it had arisen so rapidly and so dynamically, that the first generations of Christians were trying to find ways to define what it was. Notably, Peter also chose this imagery.

Comparing the Church to a temple would have been easy for both Jew and Gentile to grasp. The ancient world was full of temples—some large, ornate, and impressive while others were simpler buildings. To the Jews the only temple that mattered was the one that Herod had constructed in Jerusalem and unbeknownst to them, was in its final days. The point is, they could all picture a temple, and understood that it was for a consecrated purpose, built to be the focal point of worship.

Beginning with the foundation, Paul tells the readers how this new temple, this living, breathing, and organic one, was built on people. "Apostles and prophets" were mentioned first. This need not be restricted to these two offices in our understanding. "Paul is referring to the broader activity of those ministering in Jesus' name by way of spiritual gifts as described in Ephesians 4:11."[19] This is more than some sort of mosaic made up of various humans, but it is their message as well. The people involved only have their meaning in the message that they bear. It is not only the message of salvation, but holiness, service, devotion, discipline, biblical knowledge, and principles—the stuff that forms our spiritual muscle so we can live, fight, and persevere with the life that is ours in Christ.

The Chief Cornerstone

Next, Paul spoke of "Christ himself as the chief cornerstone" (v 20). The theme of Christ not only being the cornerstone, but the one that the "builders had rejected," is woven throughout the New Testament. There is some discussion among scholars as to whether this should be cornerstone or capstone. If the cornerstone, then it means that everything aligns to Him, just as the walls of a building are set and aligned to a cornerstone. If a capstone, it carries the idea of the stone that is center in the arch, that holds all the other stones in place. In that the Romans popularized the arch, this latter interpretation may carry more weight. Regardless, our Lord is the one who aligns everything correctly in the Church and in our living.

From His key position, Paul said that in Jesus a holy temple, *the* holy temple that is His body, allows everything to be joined together. In Herod's Temple, as with Solomon's, the stones were carefully crafted so that they fit together with precision. Looking at the Church, we don't see that kind of precision in that we are all different and the Lord loves us, saves us, and places us as building stones in His temple. So, rather than picturing perfectly sculpted stones, we ought to see ourselves as loads of boulders, pebbles, slivers, and rubble that God, through His wondrous grace, *causes* to fit together into something more beautiful, more magnificent, more awe inspiring than the architect's greatest design.

This is what Paul means when he concludes this section, "And in him you too are being built together to become a dwelling in which God lives by his Spirit" (v 22). In Ephesians chapter 2, we started out dead. At the end of it, we are transformed a dwelling place where God lives. Hallelujah!

DISCUSSION QUESTIONS

1) What does it mean to have our status upgraded from being strangers and foreigners in the Kingdom of God?

2) How does the metaphor of being a temple help us understand our role in the Kingdom of God?

3) Do you feel like you fit in, as part of God's temple? Why or why not?

11

THE MYSTERY OF CHRIST—A JEWISH PERSPECTIVE

EPHESIANS 3:1-6

"For this reason I, Paul, the prisoner of Christ Jesus for the sake of you Gentiles—surely you have heard about the administration of God's grace that was given to me for you, that is, the mystery made known to me by revelation, as I have already written briefly. In reading this, then, you will be able to understand my insight into the mystery of Christ, which was not made known to people in other generations as it has now been revealed by the Spirit to God's holy apostles and prophets. This mystery is that through the gospel

the Gentiles are heirs together with Israel,
members together of one body, and sharers
together in the promise in Christ Jesus."

Although we have already discussed some of
the aspects of the integration of Jews and Gentiles
in the Church, this is a major theme of Ephesians.
Because Paul keeps coming back to it, we explore it
a little further.

Mixed Motives

Evangelism was part of what fueled the exploration of the New World, the exploration of Africa as
well as sending countless thousands to the distant
shores of Asia and the Pacific. Not only did thousands go, but thousands upon thousands died, not so
much from the hostility of the receiving peoples as
the rigors of adapting to living conditions and unknown diseases. While seeking to reach unreached
people with the gospel, unfortunately there were
often other, less honorable, motives as well. Nations
were seeking new markets for their goods, resources
(including people) to be exploited. Too often the
point of reaching people was to make them miniature Europeans, in the process destroying or dam-

aging cultures, languages, and sometimes whole people groups. Frequently, reaching them meant making them like "us," rather than helping them discover their new identities in Christ while retaining aspects of their culture that are not contrary to biblical standards.

The problem was nothing new. There is an assumption called ethnocentrism that dictates that "our way is best, and you'll abandon your way as soon as you understand that." Paul dealt with this regarding the Jews. When the doors of the Church were opened to the Gentiles, no doubt that first generation of believers never expected so many Gentile converts or Gentiles would come into a relationship with Christ not ready to drop their cultures and become Jewish. We know that a sect called the Judaizers steadfastly refused to accept that salvation did not also include the requirement to become Jews in every respect, albeit with a belief in Christ as the Messiah.

The Jewish Christian Dilemma

The dilemma facing the Jewish Christians is completely understandable. For centuries they had been taught to observe the feasts and the sacrifices, dietary laws, and a host of other laws that reached the most intimate details of their lives. Their obedience to these laws could be slavish but for many they were deeply meaningful. Through Israel's ascent and decline and its place as a subjected people, the law had remained constant. It served as much a source of security as a way of life. They learned that all that had been ingrained in them was now relegated to the past. It was no longer needed because all had been fulfilled in Christ.

Exchanging the Virtual for the Real

Imagine you are a soldier deployed to the other side of the world. At home is a beautiful, six-year-old daughter who loves and adores you. For months you will be separated but through the wonder of technology you can connect via live video. There she is. You hear her voice while listening to her chatter. It is a perfect representation of her, but it is not her. In the same moment, you would feel both close to her and far away. Now the day comes when you go back home. At the airbase, you sweep her up, feel her little arms around you and the warmth of her cheek against yours. Imagine next that when you get home, she doesn't want to talk to you directly but through a video link! The video was good when there was nothing better, but now she is present with you. The video is a nuisance, far inferior to the actual presence.

For many Jews who had become accustomed to the "video" of the religious law and ceremony, there was great joy in the actual presence of Christ. They understood it was time to set the second-best aside. But after knowing nothing but the video of the law, it was going to take some getting used to.

Thrown Together

And now the room was crowded with all these other people who spoke, ate, and thought different- ly, but who were hugging the same Messiah you and your people waited so long to see. But when your resentment began to rise, you realized that this was the way it was always meant to be. He came for you, yes. But He also came for them.

How was all this going to work together? Why hadn't they seen it all along? That is why Paul calls it a mystery, not in the sense of a whodunit but in something being revealed that had never been un- derstood before, and which *only God could reveal*. There is no way they would have seen this coming if God did not reveal it. That makes it all the more spectacular.

The God who had given the law and the ceremo- nies did so to signal a greater reality was coming, with a greater scope than they could have imagined, accomplishing a greater purpose than the universe could have anticipated. That which had been irreconcilable would be knit together in the Church.

What was cast as the reconciliation of all nature when Christ comes to reign again on earth also had application in the rupture in humankind caused by sin and witnessed in the animosity between Jew and Gentile before Christ ruled in their hearts: "The wolf will live with the lamb, the leopard will lie down with the goat, the calf and the lion and the yearling together; and a little child will lead them" (Isaiah 11:6). In Christ, warring ground has become the place for picnics; prey and predator have become playmates; Jews and Gentiles have become the new people of God.

DISCUSSION QUESTIONS

1) How can our cultural bias get in the way of our fellowship as believers?

2) How does the video illustration help us understand the reality that Christ brought into the world when He came?

3) Can you think of any other mysteries that Christ revealed when He came? Could they have been known any other way except by God's revelation?

12

THE MYSTERY OF CHRIST—A GENTILE PERSPECTIVE

EPHESIANS 3:1-6

"For this reason I, Paul, the prisoner of Christ Jesus for the sake of you Gentiles—surely you have heard about the administration of God's grace that was given to me for you, that is, the mystery made known to me by revelation, as I have already written briefly. In reading this, then, you will be able to understand my insight into the mystery of Christ, which was not made known to people in other generations as it has now been revealed by the Spirit to God's holy apostles and prophets. This mystery is that through the gospel

the Gentiles are heirs together with Israel,
members together of one body, and sharers
together in the promise in Christ Jesus."

The Cost

As the Apostle Paul continues his explanation of this quantum shift that has occurred, he now directs his remarks to the Gentile believers. He reminds them that this message has come with a price. Not only did it result in the crucifixion of Christ, but there was a personal cost for Paul as well—it was his freedom.

Note how Paul refers to himself: "the prisoner of Christ Jesus." As William Barclay points out, "Paul never thought of himself as the prisoner of Rome: he always thought of himself as a prisoner of Christ."[20] F.R. Maltby adds that Jesus promised His disciples three things—"they would be absurdly happy, completely fearless and in constant trouble." Knowing this, the believer can never be defeated. Those who went after Paul certainly were not trying to do him any favors or expand his ministry by having him locked up. As with Jesus, they thought they were putting a lid on the problem when they took him out of circulation.

The man or woman of God who fully trusts God with his or her way will never find themselves in the wrong place. No matter how intent our enemies are to harm us, they cannot place us anywhere that God can't use for His glory. This is not to say that they are not responsible for their evil intentions and acts. Unless they seek God's forgiveness, they will be held accountable. But just as Paul did not ever consider himself to be a prisoner of Rome but rather a "prisoner of Christ Jesus," if you trust Him to use you where you are *regardless of who put you there*, then you will never be defeated. Is it a prison for Paul? Then there are letters to be written, the faith to be explained. Does the prison door fly open? Then there are places to visit and a gospel to proclaim.

Shared Inheritance

Paul goes on to speak further of this mystery of the Gentiles given access to the same inheritance as the Jews, as together they now form the Church. Again, it is not a mystery like Agatha Christie would write but the revelation of something that could not be arrived at by human reasoning. It had to be revealed by God Himself.

The Gentiles are "heirs together" (v 6) with the Jews. Did it mean that a Gentile could claim something when a Jewish parent died, and that his estate would be divided among his natural children? Did it mean that a Gentile could now claim a plot in the Promised Land? Not at all. The Gentiles becoming heirs with the Jews did not diminish one iota of what the Jews had promised to them. This was not a case of a game of divine take away.

Welcome to the Family

Rather, Gentiles became heirs because the family of God was expanded to include them. Just as the firstborn child does not become less the daughter or son when another sibling is added to the family, nor the parent is somehow more the mother or father to the fifth child than the fourth child, God's family wondrously expands to receive more children regardless of how many there are. So, you can say that God is your Father and so can I. He is as much my Father as yours, and no less yours than He is mine.

With an infinite Kingdom of measureless resources, there is never any need to squabble over who gets what. My answer to prayer does not mean I received today's quota and there won't be anything left for you. Your blessing doesn't mean that I'm left with leftovers to scrape by on. We are heirs together, fully blessed and endowed.

Paul helps us to understand that this is part of the mystery that has been revealed. There is plenty of salvation for everyone, plenty of blessing for all who are in Christ, plenty of eternity to fill all of our forevers.

Tony Evans shares the following illustration that might be helpful:

> "Many people grew up watching *The Beverly Hillbillies* —Jed Clampett, Elly May and Jethro. That was a fun show about folks trying to get used to being rich. These folks didn't know how to act when they discovered how rich they were.
>
> So, here's a question. Jed Clampett one day hit black gold. He hit oil. How long had Jed Clampett been a millionaire? Did he become a millionaire on that day he inadvertently came across the fact that there was oil, or had he been a millionaire and just was an uninformed one? There are a lot of spiritual Jed Clampetts walking around today who have untold of which they are unaware."[21]

Most of us who read this are Gentiles by birth but the fully endowed children of our Heavenly Father by the new birth in Christ. We are rich.

DISCUSSION QUESTIONS

1) In what way is God using you in your current circumstances? Would it be as possible had you not been where you are now?

2) Given that we are joint heirs with Christ, why do you think jealousy exists among believers?

3) How are you failing to realize how rich you are in Christ?

13

A SERVANT OF THIS GOSPEL

EPHESIANS 3:7-13

"I became a servant of this gospel by the gift of God's grace given me through the working of his power. Although I am less than the least of all the Lord's people, this grace was given me: to preach to the Gentiles the boundless riches of Christ, and to make plain to everyone the administration of this mystery, which for ages past was kept hidden in God, who created all things. His intent was that now, through the church, the manifold wisdom of God should be made known to the rulers and authorities in the heavenly realms, according to his eternal purpose that he accomplished in Christ Jesus our Lord. In him

*and through faith in him we may approach
God with freedom and confidence. I ask you,
therefore, not to be discouraged because of
my sufferings for you, which are your glory."*

Unselfish Service

Princess Alice, the daughter of Queen Victoria,
had a little boy who was deathly ill with diphtheria. Highly contagious, he was quarantined, even
his mother refusing admittance to him. She tried to
stay away but her heart broke when she heard him
whisper to his nurse, "Why doesn't my mother kiss
me anymore?" Running to her son, she scooped him
up in her arms and covered him with kisses. In a
few days, both she and her son were dead. Love can
cost dearly.[22]

Grace Given

Paul shared that his love for the Lord that was
shown to the Gentiles had cost him a great deal, but
he also considered it a great gift. He said he became
a servant of this gospel "by the gift of God's grace
given me through the working of his power" (v
7). He repeated that grace was given to him even
though he was "less than the least of all the Lord's

people" (v 8). No doubt, whenever Paul thought about grace or if he was the least tempted to begin to think too highly of himself, he remembered the man that he had been. Although very religious, he was also murderous. Before, as with others through history, the zeal he had considered love for God allowed for violence against His creatures. "The end justifies the means" has been the catch phrase for oceans of sin. "What kind of a man was I to have done such a thing?" Paul must have pondered countless times. The answer was frightening, "I am the kind of man who would do such a thing." We all want to be known for the best that we are but re-calling what we could be, or were, without the grace of God puts things into perspective. It did for Paul. While the Church was grateful and honored him for his leadership and his ministry, he only offered, "I am less than the least of the Lord's people" (v 8).

Although. All that may have been true, but Paul was still allowed to preach the precious gospel of Christ. *Although*. That same word stands like a great signpost that marks the parting of the way between the days of sin and the days of grace. Rather than looking at what disqualifies us, we look to what makes us able. *Although* … is the grace of God.

A Great River

The mystery of the Church was not only something for the first generation to ponder. It is not only that Gentiles and Jews are blended in a great river of salvation but that in each generation there are tributaries that continue to flow. Here is one whose family stretching back to unknown generations worshipped ancestors but now kneels at the feet of Christ. Here is another who may have smugly believed his parents' righteousness was enough to excuse him from his personal commitment until the day he sees the wretchedness of his own heart and knows his need for divine forgiveness. Here is another who has lived her life in a vacuum, blown by the winds of culture and education and popular opinion. She lives in some mishmash of platitudes and sappy sentiment until that day when reality rudely bursts her bubble. She needs the real answers that come only from Christ, and she finds Him. These blend in the streams that form the Church, a mystery as wondrous as the brotherhood that formed between the Jewish and the Gentile believers.

Not that forming an organization was the end product, but the Church has become that instrument that God uses to work in the world. Yes, it is flawed—as flawed as the individuals who comprise it. But in His eyes, it is something beautiful, something as useful as a body is to a person.

His Eternal Purpose

Paul reminds us that God is using the Church, "according to his eternal purpose that he accomplished in Christ Jesus our Lord. In him and through faith in him we may approach God with freedom and confidence" (vv 11-12). The river that is the Church has its energy and flows for the purpose of bringing us near to God. Staggering.

The apostle then circled around to himself. Don't be discouraged about what I am going through, he said. It is like he was standing on some high peak and before him in spectacular grandeur was the vista of seeing God moving in the world. And he had a part in it. And you have a part in it, too. It is worth whatever it costs—the scraped knees, the broken bones, the exhaustion and the wear and tear. Don't be discouraged for me. All this, said Paul, is for your glory (v 13).

DISCUSSION QUESTIONS

1) How does Paul seeing himself as the "least of all the Lord's people" apply to your life?

2) The author says that the influx of people over the ages is akin to the Jews and Gentiles forming the Church. Why or why not is this accurate?

3) In what ways does God use the Church, His body, to serve His purpose in the world?

14

POWER THROUGH HIS SPIRIT (PART 1)

EPHESIANS 3:14-19

"For this reason I kneel before the Father, from whom every family in heaven and on earth derives its name. I pray that out of his glorious riches he may strengthen you with power through his Spirit in your inner being, so that Christ may dwell in your hearts through faith. And I pray that you, being rooted and established in love, may have power, together with all the Lord's holy people, to grasp how wide and long and high and deep is the love of Christ, and to know this love that surpasses knowledge—that you may be filled to the measure of all the fullness of God."

Lessons from Infants

There are few things more wondrous than the birth of a child. Even the most emotionally detached person must take a moment to look at a newborn, pause, and admire when a baby appears. The parents find that all attempts to describe how they feel are lost in a sea of tears. Mothers instinctively check the baby from head to toe while fathers find their own instincts to protect are at a new height. There in that little package is everything it takes to be a human being.

Contrast that with different species in the animal kingdom. Many animals lay their eggs and leave them to their own devices. Then there are others who, while guarding their eggs as they gestate, begin to eat all the young they can grab as soon as the babies are born, leaving the children to run for their lives. Still other species, jealously nurture their infants but at a given moment, drive them away to fend for themselves.

Humans are remarkably different. God made us to understand that the moment of birth is not the end of our responsibility for the child, but the beginning. The child senses her dependence as well, looking to her parents for protection and provision, answers to questions, and reassurance as she learns. Many times, what parents know is best for the child is not what the child wants. There is food he would rather not eat, visits to the doctor that are painful to areas he would rather not have touched, rules that he would rather ignore, and denials to things he is absolutely sure he *must* have.

Growing in Christ

In addressing the Ephesians, Paul hit on a wide range of subjects. He has spoken of their hopelessness in sin, the breathless provision of grace that is the basis for our relationship with God and the lifeblood of our continued life in Him. He has helped them understand that their relationship with God has also spawned a new relationship with other people, some of whom he would have avoided at all costs were it not for the work of God in them and their fellow believers. In this prayer, he brought before them what must happen in their inner lives. As a child is not finished at the point of her birth, so much more must happen in the life of the person in Christ as they go along in their journey. It is definitely not a "one and done" kind of salvation, any more than you feed a baby one time and that meal will sustain him for eighteen years.

Paul shared, "I kneel before the Father" (v 14).

Interestingly, this is the only time Paul referenced his posture while praying. It was a departure from what was the normal practice in these days, when people stood, lifting their faces heavenward with their arms outstretched. Kneeling was the act of total submission. We can certainly speak to the Lord in any manner, however the idea of the humility that comes with kneeling is to be noted. When he was the roaring Saul of Tarsus, breathing his threats as he traveled toward Damascus, kneeling in submission would never have crossed his mind. But God had done a work in him that produced a different mind reflecting a different heart. He had gone from an attitude of "fill my hands," to a plea of "receive my gifts"; from "unleash me to fight," to "I dare not venture forth without Your help."

Our New Identity

After his discussion of the new people of God, he came back around to remind believers of their new identity. From our Father, we are the ones "from whom every family in heaven and on earth derives its name" (v 15). With few exceptions, most cultures identify people by two names: their family name and their given name. In most Western cultures, the last name is the family name that describes who we are not only in the context of our immediate family, but also in the link between the generations that have gone before us and the ones that will come after us.

When our Father gives us our family name, He sets us in context. We do not live to ourselves. We are part of the generations of believers who have gone before us, and if we do as we ought in seeking to win others, we will be that link between the centuries and the future generations of believers that follow.

That tie to others is based on our relationship to God as our Father. We may be paupers here, weak, unknown, and unnoticed, but we are especially loved by the Father who connects us to His riches. We have His account to draw on as we go, His resources to fortify us as we grow, His wealth that promises that this river will never run dry.

DISCUSSION QUESTIONS

1) How does comparing our Christian life with children growing up help us understand our need?

2) How much does attitude matter when we come to God in prayer?

3) You have a new family name when you are in Christ. What does that mean to you?

15

POWER THROUGH HIS
SPIRIT (PART 2)

EPHESIANS 3:14-19

*"For this reason I kneel before the Father, from
whom every family in heaven and on earth
derives its name. I pray that out of his glorious
riches he may strengthen you with power through
his Spirit in your inner being, so that Christ may
dwell in your hearts through faith. And I pray
that you, being rooted and established in love,
may have power, together with all the Lord's holy
people, to grasp how wide and long and high
and deep is the love of Christ, and to know this
love that surpasses knowledge—that you may be
filled to the measure of all the fullness of God."*

Among the most eloquent prayers of the Bible, this one is more than poetry. Paul brought to God specific, vital requests for believers.

Strengthen You with Power Through His Spirit

Boasting and oneupmanship were integral to life in the ancient world. Every interaction, personal, professional, in sports, in friendships and more so with enemies, was seen as an opportunity for a person to prove his prowess and superiority over the other guy. Personal power was lusted after and, when gained, lorded over others. Paul wanted believers to understand that, yes, power is important—he will bring it up again later in this complicated sentence. Drawing on their cultural idea, the word Paul used here for "power" is the one used for Greek wrestlers as they grappled with one another.[23] Wrestlers in those days often died from the struggle, so this is a call for the power needed for life and death struggles. But it is not the power that comes from flexing muscles or pounding on chests. This is a power greater than any person can produce from his or her natural abilities. It is found solely in the Holy Spirit.

These people well knew what it was to in one moment triumph in a business transaction, then fall prey to a petty temptation. They knew what it was to boast of their physical strength but then cower when they should speak for the Lord. Mental and physical skills worked well in their place, but they were not enough to live a holy life. A holy life needs the Holy Spirit, needs His power that surges forth in godly action in the crucial moment. The greatest physical weakling can stand like a lion when God gives him the roar.

Christ Might Dwell in Your Heart through Faith

The Jewish believers had a solid idea of God being present with them, as expressed in numerous places. "Even though I walk through the darkest valley, I will fear no evil, for you are with me" (Psalm 23:4); "My presence shall go with you, and I will give you rest" (Exodus 33:14); "Be strong and courageous. Do not fear or be in dread of them, for it is the Lord your God who goes with you" (Deuteronomy 31:6). But the presence of God was something outside the person. He could sense God near but not in his heart.

What was so different with the coming of the Holy Spirit at Pentecost was that now the Spirit of God came to dwell with the person internally on an ongoing basis. He is not out there somewhere. Rather, He is in here, with me, empowering, guiding, purifying, and guarding me. That changes everything.

How does such a thing happen? By faith we believe that He who cannot be contained by a million galaxies can yet find a place in my heart. I can say by faith that the Lord is in my heart, not to boast, but to wonder that it is so.

Rooted and Established in Love

Love was the distinguishing mark of the early Church. Tertullian, an early Church Father, in his defense of Christians, summed up how believers were viewed begrudgingly by unbelievers: "See how these Christians love one another!"[24] Jesus, in His parting words before His crucifixion, underscored the importance of love for fellow believers, "By this everyone will know that you are my disciples, if you love one another" (John 13:35).

While we are to love the Lord supremely (Matthew 22:37-40), this is inseparable from our love for each other. The Apostle John made the connection unmistakably clear: "Whoever claims to love God yet hates a brother or sister is a liar. For whoever does not love their brother and sister, whom they have seen, cannot love God, whom they have not seen" (1 John 4:20).

Being rooted and established in love, both for God and for each other, is what will help us weather the storms as well as grow in our faith.

Power to Grasp Surpassing Knowledge

In the summary to this section of his great prayer, Paul wished something for the believers that they never can fully have. He spoke of their power to grasp the full breadth and depth of what Christ's love is—an impossibility for us with minds too small and hearts too limited. If God fully showed us how great the love of Christ is, our hearts would burst wide, unable to take it all in. We would strangle to gasp for breath if He revealed how expansive His love is. But we can have glimpses, moments when we touch the borderline of eternity and feel ourselves taken in.

Like standing on the seashore in England and trying to spy the seashore of the Atlantic in Canada, we cannot possibly see the fullness of the love of Christ. It is as impossible as looking into the skies through a telescope to see the far place where the universe ends as to fathom all that is contained in the love of Christ. It is as hopeless as thinking we could make ourselves small enough to trace the atoms with our fingertips to explore the detail of the

love of Christ as it is shown even in our own lives.
Well we remember the old gospel song that says,

Could we with ink the ocean fill,
And were the skies of parchment made,
Were every stalk on earth a quill,
And every man a scribe by trade;
To write the love of God above
Would drain the ocean dry;
Nor could the scroll contain the whole,
Though stretched from sky to sky.

—Frederick M. Lehman [25]

DISCUSSION QUESTIONS

1) How vital is God's power in the life of the believer?

2) Think about God's presence. How can you explain that to an unbeliever?

3) Why is love for each other necessary if we say we love God?

4) Why would Paul tell us to grasp something we cannot possibly hold?

16

IMMEASURABLY MORE

EPHESIANS 3:20,21

"Now to Him who is able to do immeasurably more than all we ask or imagine, according to his power that is at work within us, to him be glory in the church and in Christ Jesus throughout all generations, for ever and ever! Amen."

Overwhelming

Our tendency is to turn away from things that overwhelm us. If we owe a huge debt, we want to quit thinking about it. When the sun is too bright, we instinctively shield our eyes. When life's pressures build up, we want to step away, sometimes to gather ourselves but at other times to escape it altogether. If we allow our minds to ponder how insignificantly small we are compared to the galaxy or the expanses of space, we know at once that it is too much to conceive and so we must stop after a few moments. When considering God, the atheist simply has given up because the very existence of the eternal, all-powerful, all-knowing God is too fantastic for his mind to grasp. Not that any of us can fully grasp it. Though we may believe, we focus on the here and now of God in our lives because here He proves Himself to be very real, very tangible. We know Him in the little bits that are within that we can hold and see and experience. Fortunately, as the psalmist says, "He knows how we are formed, he remembers that we are dust" (Psalm 103:14).

But even the things close at hand are staggering. Whether we are believers or not, we all benefit from what is known as "common grace." Jesus referred to this when He said that "he causes his sun to rise on the evil and the good and sends rain on the righteous and the unrighteous" (Matthew 5:45). There are blessings that are ours simply because we are humans.

Human Example

Take, for example, verbal communication. A thought in your mind is channeled into words. Your mind tells your body to share this physically. Air in your lungs pushes into your throat, across tiny vocal cords and then into your mouth. By manipulating your tongue, sometimes against your teeth and sometimes by rapid movements, the air is pushed out through your lips where more movements shape the sound. The air then pushes out in front of you in sound waves that travel some distance until those waves reach someone else's ears. More vibrations occur in the receiving ears and signals are sent to the brain that unscrambles all of this so that the receiver now knows what originated in your mind only a short moment ago. And then it is reversed so that you now receive a message from that person to you. How does this even happen? If you slow down and think about it, it is a cause for wonder. Yet, we do this every day, multiple times with a variety of people.

If we broke down the wonders of sight, of the weather cycle, of plants transforming inedible dirt into luscious fruit, or millions, *billions* of other marvels in this very moment happening all around us we already are overwhelmed thinking of all that our God is doing, not just for the ones who worship

Him but for the whole of humanity.

But Paul is being more specific. To those who have turned their lives over to Him, who name and honor Him as Lord, Paul gloried in "him who is able to do immeasurably more than all we ask or imagine, according to his power that is at work within us" (v 20).

Wealth Beyond Riches

All the blessings that belong to all humanity remain ours as well, but now there is another layer of blessing that is the wealth of the child of God. In Christ we have stepped into a relationship and a world that has vast wonders inconceivable apart from Him. Paul has already talked about us having been dead. Our graveyards testify to the finality of death but in Christ these dead souls of ours not only found life, but an abundant life. These bodies that serve us one moment then betray us the next are destined to be transformed into what they were meant to be from the beginning when we walk with Him on the redeemed earth. Already in Christ we see and understand things that the unredeemed cannot know, we love what otherwise we could not love, we find joy where logically only despair should be.

The moment a person receives Christ as Savior, that new life is more than an upgrade—it is a total transformation. And it keeps coming. Each day a believer wakes up is a day when God will show Himself to be present. In each experience, whether good or bad, God is near His child. We don't know the grace we will need for tomorrow, but God does, and He is ready for us in that moment to do "immeasurably more than we could ask or imagine." Paul is reminding us that if we number our blessings, we will run out of numbers before God exhausts what He has for us.

No wonder he says, "to him be glory in the church and in Christ Jesus throughout all generations, for ever and ever!" (v 21). How can we not give Him glory? How can we not bow down in utter gratitude? How can we not proclaim His praise throughout all generations, forever and ever?

DISCUSSION QUESTIONS

1) How does it make you feel when you think of God's greatness?

2) The author speaks of common grace. What other instances of common grace can you think of? How might these lead to someone becoming a believer?

3) In what areas of your life do you see God doing "immeasurably more" than you ask or imagine?

17

A LIFE WORTHY

EPHESIANS 4:1-8

"As a prisoner for the Lord, then, I urge you to live a life worthy of the calling you have received. Be completely humble and gentle; be patient, bearing with one another in love. Make every effort to keep the unity of the Spirit through the bond of peace. There is one body and one Spirit, just as you were called to one hope when you were called; one Lord, one faith, one baptism; one God and Father of all, who is over all and through all and in all. But to each one of us grace has been given as Christ apportioned it."

A Prisoner for the Lord

There are several places in Paul's letters where he made it a point to talk about his status as a prisoner. In none of these did he see himself as a prisoner of the Romans or a prisoner of the Jewish leaders who had conspired against him. Rather, as he stated here, he was "a prisoner for the Lord." That can be understood two ways, both of which are applicable. He was a prisoner because of the stand he took for Christ and in doing so he identified with his Lord who had been tried, arrested, and brutally crucified. In a sense he was saying, "Jesus did this for me. I am honored that I can do this for Him." The second way we can understand it was that no person, institution, or government could define for Paul what his status was. Being in Christ is always our true identity—any other conferred on us, whether complimentary or condemning, is secondary and in the end, temporary.

A Life Worthy

Paul then urged the Ephesians to "live a life worthy of the calling you have received" (v 1). This is a general call to all believers, not a specific call to vocational ministry. No believer can escape this obligation.

What does it mean to walk worthy? How can anyone be worthy in God's sight?

This is not to make ourselves worthy by our actions. Rather, it is to live up to what it means to be a follower of Christ. Paul worked through what it means to be part of the new people of God, a different people made so by their redemption and the new laws that govern their living. Walking worthy means we realize we are no longer a part of this worldly system since our citizenship is in Heaven. But it also means that as believers we are to be faithful in how we handle the responsibilities that God has given us, how we use the gifts that His Spirit reveals in us, how we apply ourselves to the opportunities that arise for our witness. If someone points to us and says, "She is a Christian," no one should be surprised to hear it because what we are in our words and actions spoke of it long before someone put it into words.

How We Behave Toward Each Other

Paul further defined what this meant by outlining several aspects of the life that is now ours.

Humble: Humility was a trait despised by both the Greeks and the Romans. It is accurate to say that humility as a positive trait was unknown before Christianity. It does not mean to grovel or say negative things about ourselves. It means that we do not assert ourselves or our rights at the expense of others, that we actively seek the wellbeing of another person without expecting that they return the favor. William Barclay further helps us: "True humility comes when we face ourselves, when we see our own weakness, our own selfishness, our own failure in work and in personal relationships and achievement."[26]

Gentle: The original word in Greek referred to the domestication of animals, so that while not sacrificing their strength, they submitted their strength to a harness for a good purpose. It means to have self-control in exasperating circumstances or with difficult people.

Patient: Barclay tells us that this is to have "tolerance in a relationship." It is a spirit that never gives in; even when the opportunity comes for revenge against someone who has wronged us, we do not exercise that power.[27]

Love: Paul's famous exposition about love in 1 Corinthians 13 shows us the utter unselfishness of love, its heart set on the one who is loved and desire for that other person to flourish. Love finds joy in the simplest things, from a child's smile to a gentle touch. It does not discriminate. The one whom the world makes its whipping boy can find that in the Christian, he is loved and valued.

Peace: To be with people is to experience friction. I remember well being wisely counseled by one of my leaders who said, "We are swimming in a small pool. We're bound to run into each other." But the peace that Paul spoke of finds a way to defuse conflicts and establish understanding. It is to seek a right relationship with other people, to recognize and set aside our own pettiness in the interest of others. It results in a bond that creates unity.

One

Paul outlined what this unity looks like. One body, Spirit, Lord, faith, baptism, God and Father who is "over all and through and in all" (v 4–5). While it might be helpful to break down each of these, Paul's point was that when we follow these heart rules in the household of faith, we will find that we are united on every essential point. It does not mean we don't see things differently or work differently, but in doing so, we do not forget that we are one in Christ. It is remembering that we are destined for a life when this earthly body fails us; in our continuing life in the presence of God our differences will be left behind in the coffin with our bodies.

DISCUSSION QUESTIONS

1) How does Paul's view of himself as a prisoner of Christ apply to where you are in life?

2) Do you live a life "worthy of the calling you have received"? Why or why not?

3) Among the traits that Paul outlines for the believer, which one is the hardest for you to live out? What stands in the way?

18

HE GAVE SOME

EPHESIANS 4:8-13

"This is why it says:
'When he ascended on high,
He took many captives
and gave gifts to his people.'
(What does "he ascended" mean except
that he also descended to the lower, earthly
regions? He who descended is the very
one who ascended higher than all the
heavens, in order to fill the whole universe.)
So Christ himself gave the apostles, the
prophets, the evangelists, the pastors and
teachers, to equip his people for works
of service, so that the body of Christ may
be built up until we all reach unity in the

faith and in the knowledge of the Son of God and become mature, attaining to the whole measure of the fullness of Christ."

Tributes to Gifts

Verse eight in this passage has a fascinating twist. Paul is quoting Psalm 68:18—almost. In its original context in Psalms it says, "When you ascended on high, you took many captives; you received gifts *from* people" (italics added). Paul presented the verse as, "When he ascended on high, he took many captives and gave gifts *to* his people." In the Old Testament view of the Lord, He is receiving tributes from the conquered people. But in this setting, rather than receiving tribute, the Lord is distributing what is His to those He loves. This is more than a subtle change of predicates. It gives new meaning to how things work in God's economy.

While we still owe the Lord our tribute, as happened in ancient times, Caesar shared the treasure from conquest with the soldiers who had borne the battle. God rewards His children. But maybe not in the way people might first expect.

Gifts that Give

The heresy of the prosperity gospel takes verses like this to portray God as some grand casino where every pull of the one-armed bandit results in a jackpot. If you don't get the jackpot, there's something wrong with your faith. This blasphemy makes God the servant and the believer the master.

But if we keep reading past this one change that the Holy Spirit inspired Paul to make, we find what God is giving is not bulging wallets or soaring investments. Rather, He is giving the believer work to do. The work serves to build the Kingdom but it also builds the believer. If I am a construction worker, I labor to erect a building. At the same time, my skills increase, my muscles build up, and over time I can see what my efforts meant for the final result. Although two very different things are happening at different levels and moving toward different results, they are complementary.

The Gifts

What follows is a short listing of gifts, one of several in the New Testament. The lists should be taken from all the different resources so that when we look at them, we have a comprehensive view of how God gifts His Church. No doubt if the New

Testament was written in our current day, we would find further gifts such as IT, audio, or visual arts. God is infinitely creative in His gift giving as well as how He works through the people He has so gifted.

Here Paul mentioned four roles: apostles, prophets, evangelists, and pastors/teachers. Like the main supports of a building, the other gifts fill in around these like the walls that flank the supports to further fill out the building.

The first mentioned was the apostle. There are two different ways to view that term. In the first generation of the Church, they were the leaders who were qualified because they had actually been with Jesus and as such, had an authority having heard things directly from Christ Himself. Obviously, that could not last as they died away. So, in this sense it represents those who are gifted to administer the Church. God has hard wired humans to organize, build teams, and set down rules and procedures in order to accomplish mission. A lot of it is, frankly to most of us, boring but necessary. If you have ever flown in an airplane, you can be grateful that some people somewhere drew complex drawings and dictated that certain materials be used to make that plane safe. The pilot may get the glory but flying would be nothing but a dream were it not for those who dictated how the plane could even take off.

The next gift is the prophet. We usually think of a prophet as someone who has insight into the future, but the biblical idea is more someone who shares the mind of God to the people of God. Under the direction of the Holy Spirit, prophets were guided to provide God's direction. This is a gift that Satan loves to counterfeit, which is why the Bible also gives guidelines so we can know the true prophets from the false ones. (See Deuteronomy 18:15-22).

The third gift is that of the evangelist. Evangelists are not only headliners, like Billy Graham used to be, but people who have the unique gifting, again under the leadership of the Holy Spirit, to lead people to making a decision for Christ. All believers are to evangelize but there are some who, when they do, seem to sense the timing or say the right words in a critical moment that God blesses with visible conversions. This also includes those who are called to evangelize people and groups, or serve as church planters.

The final group is listed in our Scripture as two offices, but most commentators agree that they are dual roles by what is called the pastor/teacher. While perhaps not as flashy as some of the other gifts mentioned, the pastor/teacher's work very likely yields more fruit. Over the years I have asked all sorts of people who most influenced them in their Christian faith. Besides parents, the answers more than any other by far were a corps officer, a Sunday school teacher, or a local officer. Hardly ever did someone mention the high profile leaders, or the ones whose names appear in history books. These people are important, of course. But pastors tend to work by the daily living of a Christian's life, the quiet word of instruction or correction, the action that is mulled over in an impressionable mind.

The Why

The purpose for all these offices is "to equip His people for works of service, so that the body of Christ might be built up" (v 12). Paul further said that through their gifts we would find "unity in the faith" and "knowledge of the Son of God" that leads toward maturity. I have used the building illustration earlier in this book but if we can, let's somehow picture the building not as cold, lifeless brick and mortar but rather as a living organism that is continually growing into something better, more effective. The Church is not a monument or a landmark but, as stated elsewhere in Scripture, the very Body of Christ.

DISCUSSION QUESTIONS

1) How does Paul's rewording of Psalm 68:18 change things for believers?

2) In what ways do you see the four gifts Paul outlines at work in the Church today?

3) Who has most influenced you in your life in Christ? How did that person(s) do so?

19

GROWING UP

EPHESIANS 4:14-19

"Then we will no longer be infants, tossed back and forth by the waves, and blown here and there by every wind of teaching and by the cunning and craftiness of people in their deceitful scheming. Instead, speaking the truth in love, we will grow to become in every respect the mature body of him who is the head, that is, Christ. From him the whole body, joined and held together by every supporting ligament, grows and builds itself up in love, as each part does its work. So I tell you this, and insist on it in the Lord, that you must no longer live as the Gentiles do, in the futility of their thinking. They are darkened in their

*understanding and separated from the life of
God because of the ignorance that is in them
due to the hardening of their hearts. Having
lost all sensitivity, they have given themselves
over to sensuality so as to indulge in every
kind of impurity, and they are full of greed."*

As We Grow

Few things are more delightful than watching
a child grow from infancy into a young adult. In
many ways, we who are adults experience through
them once again the excitement of discovery, the
joy of play, the formation of personality. At each
stage of life, a child must successfully accomplish
certain tasks and in doing so, is readied for the next
stage and on to maturity. But what is cute at three
years old is not at thirteen. What we expect from an
eighteen-year-old is far different than our expectations for an eighteen-*month*-old.

Reflecting on childhood to measure spiritual
growth, Paul illustrates the range of emotions
that a child can show in a few moments, from
laughs and giggles one minute to big tears of
anger the next. As he often does, Paul mixes that
metaphor with one of a tiny ship being tossed

about by the wind and waves, blown and tossed by storms.

Concern

Paul had reason for concern. There are thousands of beliefs and cultural norms that often come along with life as a new believer. Although a person's heart may be instantly cleansed, thinking patterns are more stubborn. For the early Church, founded as it was in the womb of Judaism, those influences were extremely strong. Most of them, because they were part of the continuing revelation of God, led beautifully into the expanded knowledge that life in Christ brought. But others, such as the practices Jesus fought against with the Pharisees, were interpretations of the Law that God never intended and, when they came into the Church, were even more problematic than what they were before Christ came. A new believer, coming from a background without any vestiges of biblical knowledge or practice, could find himself easily influenced by a believer from a Jewish background who might have held on to some of these beliefs. Paul was urging the new believers not to be easily moved by these.

He refers to some of these teachers as "cunning." The original word in Greek referred to dice playing and trickery.[28] This is not accidental holdover from Judaism but rather a deliberate attempt to deceive and redirect. We are reminded of Satan's ploy with Eve in the Garden of Eden, "Did God *really* say…" (Genesis 3:1, emphasis added).

Speaking Truth in Love

The antidote to the poison of this way was "to speak the truth in love." Remember that some hold to their old beliefs with full sincerity. Rather than shame them, we are to bring them along to the fuller truth that is the gospel. Maturity in the faith, "takes away our naiveté and enables us to recognize the truth."[29] John Stott says that this means "'truthing in love' and includes living and doing the truth."[30] We cannot afford to indulge someone by allowing them to continue in their error, for their sake and for the sake of those who they might influence. Confrontation and correction can be painful but like sterilizing a wound, it is better than losing a limb because of an untreated infection.

Don't Look Back

Paul moved beyond the Jewish influences to those of the Gentile world. He reminded the Gentile believers of where they came from and how dangerous that was in "the futility of their thinking … darkened in their understanding and separated from the life of God" (v 17–18).

Perhaps in a wistful moment, a Gentile believer thought of some of the festivals from their former worship. Paul doused them with reality that all the former practices, without exception, were useless and perilous because they all led the followers of them straight off a cliff. There was no good end. Any part of the former life of unbelief that failed to bring them to God was a hurdle, a road branching in the wrong direction.

The tragedy is that those in it often fail to see it. Watch television commercials about alcohol or gambling. It's all a big game, a laugh-filled party with great friends and great times. Never depicted are the empty food cupboards, the children hiding in fear as a raging parent storms through the house, the vomit-encrusted man lying in his squalor against some abandoned building. As Merida says, "Sin produces a malfunction of the mind."[31]

It is not only desirable that a Christian grow beyond these things, but it is vital that she do so. There can be no looking back or like Lot's wife, we are stopped dead in the process (Genesis 19:26). The young convert in India, S. Sundar Singh, realized this when he wrote his song:

> *I have decided to follow Jesus;*
> *I have decided to follow Jesus;*
> *I have decided to follow Jesus;*
> *No turning back, no turning back.*
>
> *The world behind me, the cross before me;*
> *The world behind me, the cross before me;*
> *The world behind me, the cross before me;*
> *No turning back, no turning back.*
>
> *Though none go with me, still I will follow;*
> *Though none go with me, still I will follow;*
> *Though none go with me, still I will follow;*
> *No turning back, no turning back.*[32]

DISCUSSION QUESTIONS

1) What non-Christian beliefs do you sometimes see demonstrated among believers?

2) How would you go about speaking the truth in love to someone who was going the wrong direction as a Christian?

3) Why is it important to not desire life outside of Christ?

20

PUT OFF THE OLD SELF

EPHESIANS 4:20-28

"That, however, is not the way of life you learned when you heard about Christ and were taught in him in accordance with the truth that is in Jesus. You were taught, with regard to your former way of life, to put off your old self, which is being corrupted by its deceitful desires; to be made new in the attitude of your minds; and to put on the new self, created to be like God in true righteousness and holiness. Therefore each of you must put off falsehood and speak truthfully to your neighbor, for we are all members of one body. 'In your anger do not sin.' Do not let the sun go down while you are still angry, and do not give the devil a

foothold. Anyone who has been stealing must steal no longer, but must work, doing something useful with their own hands, that they may have something to share with those in need."

In Papua New Guinea, tribal warfare has been all too common going back across untold generations. Although Christianity is the common religion, unfortunately for many, it is a nominal allegiance. When grievances occur or are remembered, conflict heats up. But when there has been a sincere turning to Christ by members of the tribes, it results in a desire for peace. These occasions are marked by the tribes coming together in a great meeting where their faith in Christ is declared and a feast is held. Then, quite dramatically, the tribespeople pile their guns, spears, bows, and arrows, and set them on fire. By burning the weapons, they ensure symbolically and literally that these arsenals will not be used against each other again.

Deceitful Desires

In this passage, Paul was telling the Ephesians that it was time to put away, to burn if you will, those weapons they used against each other, that marked their lives. These are called "deceitful desires." Unfortunately, our NIV does not translate this as strongly as Paul meant it to be understood. Barclay says it is "a disposition of the soul incapable of bearing the pain of discipline."[33] But even this is not strong enough. A person who lives like this makes no attempt to hide his sin and indeed, may sin so often and so terribly that he can't even keep track of them anymore. With a mind and heart so darkened, sin is the atmosphere that he breathes, and like breathing, unless he stops to think about it, it is done without thought. Here is the person whose language is laced with profanities, whose lewd comments are made on every occasion. He is the one who believes he is being lied to because he lies so much himself. Sin has become ingrained so that one cannot talk of this person without immediately thinking of the evil actions associated with him.

Paul reminded his readers that that is precisely where they were. Satan is quick to try to draw the person back into that by reminding him of the shortcuts he had taken, the quick gratification of how he used to live.

Put Off the Old Self

Counteracting these deceitful desires is the new person we are in Christ. This putting off is not something like a New Year's resolution that we try to tweak a bit; it is a decisive and radical change that is through and through. The Church Father Origen wrote that the new believer "becomes new rather than old, whole rather than corrupt, fresh rather than enfeebled, an infant rather than an old man, eternal rather than ephemeral."[34] If a person claims to receive Christ but there is no evidence of a changed life, it makes the claim a lie.

We are to "put on the new self, created to be like God in true righteousness and holiness" (v 23). The sad truth is that too often we are hard pressed to tell the difference between how believers and nonbelievers act. They watch the same movies and television, have the same interactions on social media, tell the same jokes, and are motivated by the same greed. This is to our shame. We are to live righteous and holy lives, distinctly different than those who are without Christ. We rightly ask, if we can't tell the difference in a professing believer's life from that of a nonbeliever, is that person even a Christian? We remember the haunting words of Jesus, "Therefore everyone who confesses me before men, I will also confess him before my Father in heaven. But whoever denies me before men, I will also deny him before my Father in heaven" (Matthew 10:32–33). If we fail to live a holy life, we are denying our Lord. And He in turn, will deny us. As Merida points out, "Christians should not only live differently from unbelievers, but they should do so *for different* reasons. (Italics in original)."[35]

Anger

Making his point further, Paul mentioned a common problem: how to handle anger. He does not deny that anger exists or that it has its place. After all, when a parent sees someone attacking her child, anger fuels her response as she moves to protect the child. We ought to feel anger when we hear the name of our Lord blasphemed or see sinful behavior glorified. Anger was created by God as a valid emotion to be experienced in its proper place, as with all emotions. The problem is that we often use anger indiscriminately, to force our will or push our agenda upon another. That is why Paul says, "In your anger, *do not sin* (emphasis added)" (v 26).

How is this to be? First, anger is meant for a moment, not savored for an extended period of time. Paul limits it to the day in which it is expressed.

"Don't go to bed angry" is not only wise for married couples but all relationships. Granted, it is sometimes hard to put aside anger, especially if a situation is unresolved. While those things should not be ignored, they should be taken up when the fire of an angry moment has grown cold.

Paul warned, "Do not give the devil a foothold" (v 27). When the allied troops made their massive landings on D-Day, they assembled the largest armada that had ever sailed. They shelled the German fortifications and swept in with fighter and bomber aircrafts. Even so, the German defenses were largely in place, making the landings deadly. Still, through sheer guts and determination, a foothold was obtained. But one of the greatest fears was that the Germans would mount a counterattack and push the soldiers back into the sea. When they failed to do so in a timely manner, the foothold was expanded and in time, all of Europe was liberated. The foothold was the key to the success of the invasion.

Through our misuse of anger, the devil can gain a foothold and in doing so, like the allied armies, expand it until all our life is in ruins.

Stealing

In a similar fashion, taking what is not ours (vv 27–28) can lead to corruption our whole lives. Stealing was common in Asia Minor in the first century. Thievery was a part of life, the thief often boasting about his prowess in pulling one over on the unsuspecting, or telling of his skill in holding someone up. But as with other cultural norms, Christianity brought a new ethos.

In the biblical view, stealing was wrong because it deprived someone else of what was rightfully theirs. It was also a selfish shortcut taken because a person had shirked his responsibility.

Rather than depriving someone of what was theirs, the believer is to work honestly not only to provide for the needs of himself and his family, but to "share with those in need" (v 28). Stealing is selfish but we are called to unselfishness, to not take away from others what is theirs but to in fact, take what is ours and in a spirit of gratitude to God, give it away to someone else. No longer emptying the pockets of his victim, the former thief is to empty his pockets in giving to another.

DISCUSSION QUESTIONS

1) What does "putting off the old self" look like in your life? How are you living differently than unbelievers?

2) How do you deal with anger? How *should* you deal with anger?

3) Besides burglary, what other ways can a person steal from another person, business, or church?

21

BUILDING OTHERS

EPHESIANS 4:29-32

"Do not let any unwholesome talk come out of your mouths, but only what is helpful for building others up according to their needs, that it may benefit those who listen. And do not grieve the Holy Spirit of God, with whom you were sealed for the day of redemption. Get rid of all bitterness, rage and anger, brawling and slander, along with every form of malice. Be kind and compassionate to one another, forgiving each other, just as in Christ God forgave you."

Rabbi Joseph Telushkin, who wrote *Words that Hurt, Words that Heal*, shared how he often asked in his presentations how many people could go twenty-four hours without saying anything unkind about another person or to another person. Very few said that they could. Reflecting on that, he said,

"Those of you who can't answer yes must recognize that you have a serious problem. If you cannot go twenty-four hours without drinking liquor, you are addicted to alcohol. If you cannot go twenty-four hours without smoking, you are addicted to nicotine. Similarly, if you cannot go twenty-four hours without saying unkind words about others, then you have lost control of your tongue."[36]

Bible Warnings About Speech
The abuse of the tongue has been an age-old problem. Listen to the Old Testament:

• "Like a club or a sword or a sharp arrow is one who gives false testimony against a neighbor" (Proverbs 25:18).
• "Keep your tongue from evil and your lips

from telling lies" (Psalm 34:13).
• "Without wood a fire goes out; without a gossip a quarrel dies down" (Proverbs 26:20).

The New Testament continues the warnings:

• "When we put bits into the mouths of horses to make them obey us, we can turn the whole animal. Or take ships as an example. Although they are so large and are driven by strong winds, they are steered by a very small rudder wherever the pilot wants to go. Likewise, the tongue is a small part of the body, but it makes great boasts. Consider what a great forest is set on fire by a small spark. The tongue also is a fire, a world of evil among the parts of the body. It corrupts the whole body, sets the whole course of one's life on fire, and is itself set on fire by hell" (James 3:3–6).
• "But I tell you that every careless word that people speak, they shall give an account for it in the day of judgement" (Matthew 12:36).
• "If you want to enjoy life and see many happy days, keep your tongue from speaking evil and your lips from telling lies" (1 Peter 3:10).

The Tale of the Tongue

The struggle with the tongue has taken on a new dimension with the advent of social media. Here, unseen persons do battle across international lines. Without the benefit of seeing the reactions to their words, combatants flail away without restraint. Nor does it stop with strangers. Friends and family are similarly attacked in a public forum where participants strive for the stinger that will leave their opposite number bruised and bleeding.

While the passage above is not restricted solely to conversation, it is its main arena. Look at the negative words that Paul employed to describe the awful potential of misdirected language: unwholesome, grieve, bitterness, rage, anger, brawling, slander, and malice. It is the hall of fame of hurt. Not mentioned are the sins of lying, blasphemy, filthy jokes, innuendo, boasting, intimidation, and gossip. More could be listed. To indicate how odorous it all is, the Greek word for "unwholesome" is the same one used for rotting fruit or fish.[37] Suffice it to say that almost any sin that exists can find verbal expression beyond overt acts.

Christian Counterbalance

Our tongues are to be every bit as converted as

our souls. The believer must be marked by a different way of talking, writing, and communicating that stands in stark contrast to the interactions of unbelievers. Extroverts are tasked to rein it in, while introverts are to be on guard with what they whisper under their breath.

Paul counterbalances the destructive power of speech with what should mark the child of God.

Helpful in building others up: One of the marks of true love is the desire to see another person succeed and reach her full potential. We see this in the healthy parent's desire to raise a child to adulthood, helping that one to discover what God intends for him as well as the giftedness that is his. In the same way, we are not to see fellow believers as competitors but as people whom we support and help so that they can become all that God would have them be. There are spiritual gifts to be discerned and developed. There is instruction, moments of encouragement, not to flatter but to reinforce. And there are times of correction, shared lovingly so that the person is helped along.

Kind and compassionate: The ancient world was one of callousness toward those who were weak, boasting even when unjustified, and constant belittling, even with closest family. The idea of kindness and compassion was, especially to the Gentile believers, a new concept. Having not had it modeled, it had to be purposely learned. To be sure, conversion opened new parts of a person's hearts and gave the believer new affections. These needed to be nurtured and part of that nurturing was to encourage others to be kind and compassionate.

Forgiving each other: Again, forgiveness was not part of life for believers before coming to Christ. Grudges across generations resulted in volcanic seething within countless hearts, waiting to flame into anger when there was any slight, real or imagined. Forgiveness was a luxury few felt they could afford. To do so would put them at a disadvantage against those who carried ill feelings. A person letting his guard down could leave himself open for attack.

Paul gives the rationale for why forgiveness must take place. We are to forgive, "just as in Christ God forgave you" (v 32). Having endured the worst injustice and facing the most excruciating death, Christ cried from the cross, "Father, forgive them..." (Luke 23:34). That intercession of the Savior was not the climax of His love but the spring from which His forgiveness poured forth for all humankind. The gospel mandate includes the requirement that if we claim Christ's forgiveness, we have no choice but to forgive others, especially those in the household of faith.

The harshness of the tongue is traded for the gentle words of encouragement. The tongue lashing toward someone who has been wronged is exchanged for the quiet assurance that forgiveness has been given. The cruelty of competitive, one-upmanship bullying is abandoned for stepping back to let another flourish.

DISCUSSION QUESTIONS

1) In his book, James says the tongue is difficult to tame (James 3:7–8). Why is that so?

2) We all have had struggles with what we say. Where have you struggled?

3) How can our talk as Christians be marked by God's grace?

22

IMITATORS OF GOD

EPHESIANS 5:1-7

"Follow God's example, therefore, as dearly loved children and walk in the way of love, just as Christ loved us and gave himself up for us as a fragrant offering and sacrifice to God. But among you there must not be even a hint of sexual immorality, or of any kind of impurity, or of greed, because these are improper for God's holy people. Nor should there be obscenity, foolish talk or coarse joking, which are out of place, but rather thanksgiving. For of this you can be sure: No immoral, impure or greedy person—such a person is an idolater—has any inheritance in the kingdom of Christ and of God. Let no one deceive you with empty

words, for because of such things God's
wrath comes on those who are disobedient.
Therefore do not be partners with them."

While there might be a hundred singers in a choir, a parent finds her child and that's the one she watches. And though there may be a stage full of budding actors and actresses, the proud grandfather finds his little darling throughout the performance. At an airport, the child scans all the faces of those coming through the door until she finds her father and awaits the moment when she can fly into his arms. These are "dearly loved," as Paul means it, those who are loved as if there were not another person in existence. And I am loved by God in that way. It is as if His eyes are only on me, that He listens to hear my voice above all others, that in a crowd He runs to scoop me up and holds me close. Of course, we know God loves all His children but His love for each of us is so intense that we are loved as if no one else ever existed. As you dwell on the reality of God's love for you, His special love for you, hear what Paul says: "Follow God's example" (v 1).

Walking in Love

We are to walk in the way of love. What does that mean?

We have seen people who walk in the way of anger, finding offense in every action, reacting in rage. There are those who walk in sadness, hearing only melancholy music to their liking, repelled rather than encouraged by the joy of others. Others walk in conceit, seething when others are praised and constantly inserting themselves into situations. Then there is the way of love as Christ demonstrated, as Paul famously articulated so beautifully in 1 Corinthians 13, "Love is patient, love is kind. It does not envy, it does not boast, it is not proud. It does not dishonor others, it is not self-seeking, it is not easily angered, it keeps no record of wrongs. Love does not delight in evil but rejoices with the truth. It always protects, always trusts, always hopes, always perseveres. Love never fails" (vv 4-8).

This kind of loving is a "fragrant aroma and sacrifice to God" (v 2). Merida says, this represents "God's acceptance of a sacrifice given from a sincere and wholehearted worshipper."[38]

What Love is Not: Conduct

Because we love in this way, there is no room for those things that are cheap imitations of love or that undermine it.

At the top of the list is sexual immorality. In our present day as it was in Paul's time, immorality is accepted as the norm. When God created sex, He intended it as part of a loving relationship between a man and woman joined in marriage. In the original language, the word for immorality covers every kind of sexual sin that exists outside of marriage. But it includes some that exist within marriage, including what is now called marital rape. The point is that a Christian life that does not exhibit sexual purity is a lie.

Interestingly, greed is listed next. Most people nowadays would not put that on par with sexual sin, but the Bible sees things differently. Christians are to make money, use money as the tool it is meant to be, and make it a servant for God's glory. The problem with money and other possessions is that while we think we own *them*, too often they own *us*. The game system might be owned by a teen but when his fantasies are crowded with the images and sounds of a video game even when he is away from it, the game system owns him. When all else is pushed aside to gain more money even when there is more than enough to supply all her needs, the money owns that woman. You can fill in the blanks with all sorts of things. Jesus did say, "where your treasure is, there your heart will be also" (Matthew 6:21).

Greed centers on self—the very opposite of what Christ lived. Sexual immorality is self-gratification—the very opposite of what Christ modeled. Therefore, this conduct has no place in the person who claims to be a follower of Christ.

What Love is Not: Talk

Paul once again returned to the subject of what we say as a reflection of what we are. The list covers several verbal sins: obscenity, foolish talk, coarse joking. Obscenity has no place in the believer's life. Never can an obscene word build a better witness, but it most certainly can destroy one. Foolish talk and coarse joking not only include dirty jokes or innuendo, but also the kind of thing that is cruel and meant to embarrass another person. Good-natured joking is often beneficial, as it defuses a tense situation or helps build friendships. But the cutting, cruelly sarcastic remarks meant to hurt and humiliate are what Paul means here.

Paul further warns against those who try to deceive with "empty words" (v 6). This is a direct reference to people who dismiss or make light of the traits he has just spoken about. "Paul urges believers to distance themselves from those who preach a lenient gospel in which behavior doesn't matter."[39] Our beliefs and conduct are inseparable. If anyone scorns what Scripture declares, that is the one for whom Paul says, "God's wrath comes on those who are disobedient" (v 6).

DISCUSSION QUESTIONS

1) Being loved by God as if I am His favorite makes me _____.

2) How do you walk in love?

3) Can you think of any conduct not mentioned above that contradicts the Christian life?

23
CHILDREN OF LIGHT

EPHESIANS 5:8-14

*"For you were once darkness, but now you
are light in the Lord. Live as children of
light (for the fruit of the light consists in all
goodness, righteousness and truth) and find
out what pleases the Lord. Have nothing to
do with the fruitless deeds of darkness, but
rather expose them. It is shameful even to
mention what the disobedient do in secret.
But everything exposed by the light becomes
visible—and everything that is illuminated
becomes a light. This is why it is said:
'Wake up, sleeper,
rise from the dead,
and Christ will shine on you.'"*

Tony Evans shares a story about a bear that had been raised in a twelve-by-twelve foot cage. It was so familiar with the cage that it could walk from one end to the other with its eyes closed, turn around at the right spot, and walk to the other end without touching the bars. As the bear grew, the zookeepers decided it was time to move the bear into a larger cage, this one thirty-six-by-thirty-six feet. But when they put the bear in the new cage, it still only walked in a twelve-by-twelve square. Even though it had much more freedom and room, in its mind it was still confined to the smaller cage.[40] Paul told the believers in Ephesus that it was time they no longer walked in the darkness of their old life but in the light and freedom that was theirs in Christ.

Jesus as the Light

The idea of light versus darkness as an illustration contrasting the Christian life with the ungodly life is found throughout the New Testament. Jesus said, "I am the light of the world" (John 8:12). In the Sermon on the Mount, Jesus also compared our witness in the world to shining our light (Matthew 5:15).

Throughout the Gospel of John, the interplay between light and darkness runs throughout the book. One of the first things said about Jesus as the light of the world is in John 1:5, "The light shines in the darkness, and the darkness has not overcome it." John is even more explicit later: "Light has come into the world, but people loved darkness instead of light because their deeds were evil. Everyone who does evil hates the light and will not come into the light for fear that their deeds will be exposed" (John 3:19-20). We find echoes of this as well in 1 John.

Children of Light

Paul picked up on this idea by telling believers to "live as children of the light" (v 8). It works well in helping us understand how we are to live. Consider the characteristics of light and how they illustrate the Christian life:

Light reveals: Anyone who has stubbed his toe in a dark room knows how much he wished a light had been on! Light shows us what is hidden from us otherwise. We can see the way to go, take note of obstacles, and see if there are any dangers in our way. As children of the light, we find our way illumined to warn us of spiritual dangers and obstacles.

Light guides: When I was a teen, I recall driving on a road that was utterly desolate. The roads in that part of Florida crossed marshland where it was absolutely flat. There were few houses and streetlights were nonexistent. But at a little crossroads called Yeehaw Junction there was a single flashing yellow light. You could see it for miles. I knew if I kept that light in front of me it didn't matter how dark or how empty the landscape was. I would reach my destination because the light was guiding me.

In a similar way, the Lord is our light, guiding us. And as His lights in the world, we provide a beacon to other believers and non-believers alike; if they will follow the light we shed, they will be guided in the right direction. Are you a true light?

Light must shine to be useful: Jesus spoke of how ridiculous it was for a light to be hidden when it was meant to shine. He made it practical when He said, "You are the light of the world. A city set on a hill cannot be hidden. Nor do people light a lamp and put it under a basket, but on a stand, and it gives light to all in the house. In the same way, let your light shine before others, so that they may see your good works and give glory to your Father who is in heaven" (Matthew 5:14-16).

Dismissing Darkness

It is not surprising that many of the haunts of sin are dark. In fact, if it is a sunny day, you find that stepping in one can leave you almost blinded as your eyes struggle to adjust to the darkness. John tells us, "This is the judgment, that the Light has come into the world, and men loved the darkness rather than the Light, for their deeds were evil" (John 3:19). There are many other Scripture verses that employ darkness as a metaphor for sin. Because darkness hides, obscures, or endangers, it is a fitting way to think of sin.

Paul said we are to "have nothing to do with the fruitless deeds of darkness" (v 11). We can be in a bit of a quandary here. How can we witness to the lost if we are segregated from them? But that is not what Paul is saying. We are to be removed from the deeds but keep reaching out to the lost so we can win them.

Back during the First World War, several groups were allowed to operate among the troops at the frontlines. Representing the Christians were the Young Men's Christian Association (YMCA) and The Salvation Army. At that time, the YMCA was extremely evangelistic. Both organizations had "huts," or crude recreation centers, the best that could be managed under war conditions. But when many of the YMCA workers arrived at the front, most chose to blend in with the men. They smoked, told coarse jokes, drank, used profanity, and effectively blended in with the men. Although it seemed they were relating to the troops, in fact, they damaged their witness to the point that they were largely ineffective. As a result, seldom is there any mention of the YMCA's war service.

The Salvation Army resolved to not compromise its witness. While its workers were subjected to the same terrible conditions as everyone else, they had determined that their speech would be pure, their actions in keeping with the spirit of Christ, and their witness as consistent as they could. While they were close to the men and served them in every way possible, they remembered that they were first and foremost representatives, not so much of The Salvation Army, but of Christ. When the war ended, The Salvation Army, previously considered a band of eccentrics, was catapulted to a place of esteem and appreciation that persists to this present day.

We can never reach those in darkness by imitating darkness. We can only deal with the dark by being children of light.

DISCUSSION QUESTIONS

1) Can you think of any other characteristics of light not listed by the author? How do they represent the Christian life?

2) What other characteristics of darkness represent sin?

3) Why is the comparison between the war service of the YMCA and The Salvation Army helpful or not helpful?

24

FILLED WITH THE SPIRIT

EPHESIANS 5:15-20

"Be very careful, then, how you live—not as unwise but as wise, making the most of every opportunity, because the days are evil. Therefore do not be foolish, but understand what the Lord's will is. Do not get drunk on wine, which leads to debauchery. Instead, be filled with the Spirit, speaking to one another with psalms, hymns, and songs from the Spirit. Sing and make music from your heart to the Lord, always giving thanks to God the Father for everything, in the name of our Lord Jesus Christ."

Drunk on Wine

According to the USA's Center for Disease Control, excessive use of alcohol annually kills 140,000 people in the United States alone while costing $249 billion in lost productivity. To break that down into more understandable terms, Americans lost $2.05 for every alcoholic drink consumed, or $807 per year for every man, woman, and child.[41] These numbers only account for the use of alcohol.

When the use of illicit drugs is factored in, the annual cost in lost productivity skyrockets to over $3 trillion per year or almost $10,000 per person.[42] That is more than the combined gross domestic product (GDP) of forty-five of the fifty states in the United States. Substance abuse is strangling not only the whole country but wreaking havoc in homes, workplaces, schools, and even churches.

Paul warned the Ephesians not to live foolishly, commanding that they "not get drunk with wine, which leads to debauchery" (v 18). Gathering statistics like those cited above was impossible when he lived but even then he could see the effects of the unrestrained use of alcohol. Families were wrecked, the witness of believers damaged beyond repair. Despite Hollywood's portrayal and romanticizing of drug use, and the clever advertising of the alcohol industry, they cannot transform substance abuse purveyors from vampires to angels of light.

Filled with the Spirit

As it is today, when Ephesians was written many used alcohol to give them a few moments of transitory "happiness." But Paul reminded the believers that we find joy in the presence and filling of the Holy Spirit. We recall that when the Holy Spirit came in His fullness, He was first mistaken by observers as people binge drinking in the morning. "Peter stood up with the Eleven, raised his voice and addressed the crowd: 'Fellow Jews and all of you who live in Jerusalem, let me explain this to you; listen carefully to what I say. These people are not drunk, as you suppose. It's only nine in the morning!'" (Acts 2:14,15).

Just before Peter's declaration, the small body of believers that made up almost the entire Church had experienced a marvelous moving of God as the Holy Spirit came in power among them. Here we see what it means to be "filled with the Spirit."

Those who had been meeting behind closed, locked doors suddenly poured out into the streets of Jerusalem, only a few weeks after their Lord had been paraded in humiliation and murdered publicly.

The Holy Spirit gave them boldness in place of their fear, evidence of the filling of the Spirit.

They communicated effectively, overcoming their ignorance of language or their limited education. Evidence of the Holy Spirit filling a person is that the hurdles that might sideline him in the world's eyes, are of no account when God's mission is to be done.

In response to a single message, three thousand turned to Christ. Further evidence of the filling of the Holy Spirit came in God using the message of men to reach the hearts of the unsaved. A person filled with the Spirit is a soul-winner, not content with letting people bump into salvation as they grope in their spiritual darkness.

Further Evidence of Being Filled with the Spirit

Being filled with the Spirit shows itself not only in the outward thrust of being engaged in witnessing and winning souls, but in what God can do in the heart of the believer. While we do not have time to go into it here, the fruit of the Spirit comes naturally to the man or woman who is filled with the Spirit. We don't strive to have "love, joy, peace, forbearance, kindness, goodness, faithfulness, gentleness, and self-control" (Galatians 5:22-23) but as an apple tree cannot help but produce apples, the person filled with the Spirit can't help but display the fruit that by its presence, glorifies God. We don't put on the fruit like we adorn a Christmas tree with ornaments. This is a work of God, not a self-help plan to make ourselves godly.

Sing!

Christianity is a religion that does not restrict singing to specific individuals. Instead, many believers are encouraged to sing and make music in varied styles that reflect a variety of ethnic cultures or age groups. Like the fruit of the Spirit, it is a natural expression of what is in our hearts. Unlike the lark that sings but has no idea what it is singing, the Christian sings because she knows what God has done in her.

Singing is encouraged in passages such as this, where Paul notes that being filled with the Spirit results in "speaking to one another with psalms, hymns, and songs from the Spirit. Sing and make music from your heart to the Lord" (v 19). Some of us may croak more than make music but the finished product is not the issue. Of course, we love to hear a well presented solo that glories the Lord. But God invites our little voices to sing and to listen to the music of salvation in our hearts and minds as we walk along. It is one of the few things that we do on earth that we will continue to do in Heaven. This is our rehearsal time for the moment when we sing to the Lamb for all eternity.

Thankful

Frequently, Paul encouraged believers to be thankful. He said so as he sat in a prison with no promise of release. When a person is filled with the Spirit, he is not a prisoner to pain, disappointment, ill health, or loneliness. These are realities that we all must bear from time to time. But we are thankful through all these things. Rock, sand, and gravel can be a nuisance or perhaps serve as something to walk on. But in the right hands, they combine to form concrete from which skyscrapers, bridges, and monuments are built. God takes the circumstances of our lives and uses that material to make us into the image of Christ through the power of His Spirit. Triumphantly Paul proclaimed, "We know that in all things God works for the good of those who love him, who have been called according to his purpose" (Romans 8:28). When we learn that lesson, we find there is no end to our thankfulness.

DISCUSSION QUESTIONS

1) What does being filled with the Spirit mean to you?

2) In what ways does Christian music play a part in expressing what is in our hearts?

3) If we do not have a thankful spirit, what does it say about our Christian walk?

25

GOD'S VIEW OF MARRIAGE (PART 1)

EPHESIANS 5:21-24

*"Submit to one another out of reverence
for Christ. Wives, submit yourselves to
your own husbands as you do to the Lord.
For the husband is the head of the wife as
Christ is the head of the church, his body, of
which he is the Savior. Now as the church
submits to Christ, so also wives should
submit to their husbands in everything."*

Michael Ventura has said, "Marriage is a journey
toward an unknown destination— the discovery that
people must share not only what they don't know
about each other, but what they don't know about

themselves."[43] Navigating one of the most important of human relationships has never been easy. It's
a small wonder that Paul felt he had to address it
several times in his letters to believers.

Household Codes

In the ancient world, each culture had its own
"household code" that defined the roles and expected behaviors of the people in a home. Included
were slaves, children, wives, and husbands. In this
section, Paul addressed wives, and while to our
twenty-first century ears his remarks seem to be
oppressive toward women, in context they represent
a quantum leap forward in the way women were to
be viewed.

At this time, a woman was solely defined by her
relationship to the men in her life: she was someone's daughter, then wife, then mother. Unless she
was a widow, she wasn't seen to have her own
identity. By addressing women directly, Paul was
already doing what was not done, that is, acknowl-
edging that she was her own person who made her
own choices. Karen H. Jobes explains:

The husband and society would perceive the
wife's worship of Jesus Christ as rebellion, es-

pecially if she worshipped Christ exclusively. If the wife persisted in her new religion to the extent that others outside the household learned of it, the husband would also feel embarrassment and suffer criticism for not properly managing his household. This could seriously damage his social standing, even to the point of disqualifying him for certain honors and offices. Third, the wife's attendance at Christian worship would provide the opportunity for her to have fellowship with other Christians who possibly were not her husband's friends. Depending on the specifics of social expectations, a wife's conversion to Christ could potentially have far-reaching implications for her husband and family.[44]

With the friction created by a household divided by faith, how was the wife to act? She now owed her first allegiance, not to her husband but to Christ. Did that now mean that all the dictates of culture and family life were thrown overboard? As these situations increased with the spread of Christianity, there was desperate need for definition. This Paul was giving.

Mutual Submission

He first laid out an idea that while not so revolutionary to us, would have left many believers thun-
derstruck. "Submit to one another out of reverence
for Christ" (v 21). The notion that a man would
submit to his wife under any circumstances was
unheard of. No doubt, most husbands listened to
their wives, particularly when they faced the overwhelming situations that confronted them as they
lived their lives. But to submit to them? He would
have effectively surrendered his manhood.

Here we need to remember that the gospel also
introduced another foreign idea: humility. Although
humility was not unknown, it was seen as a sign
of weakness in the unbelieving world. But among
Christians, it was considered one of the crown jewels
of following Christ. Humility allows us to hear where
before we might have been deaf. It allows us to
receive what formerly we would have pushed away.
And in a marriage, it opens levels of relationship that
are barred to the couple without it. Humility is necessary for mutual submission to have any chance.

Submission by the Wife

Why then did Paul say next, "Wives, submit yourselves to your own husbands as you do to the Lord"

in verse 22? While mutual submission is in play, there are times when the husband and wife cannot reach an agreement. In those instances, I believe Paul is recommending that a wife submit to her husband in the same spirit she has submitted herself to the Lord. That is, willingly and without a bitter spirit. There must be a way to break the deadlock, and this is the God-honoring way to do so.

It is important to point out that the submission that a woman yields to her husband does not translate to all the men in her life. It is exclusive to the husband. No other man has the right to demand submission from a woman based on this or any other Scripture. Outside of the marriage relationship, a woman is free to exercise authority over others regardless of what their gender is.

In her submission, a wife witnesses to the grace of God in her life, particularly important if the husband is an unbeliever. William Barclay has written, "The silent preaching of the loveliness of her life must break down the barriers of prejudice and hostility and win her husband for the Master... it is the submission which, as someone has finely put it, is a 'voluntary selflessness,' the abasing of self, and the instinctive desire to serve, it is not the submission of fear, but the submission of perfect love."[45]

The Church

Paul took advantage of the powerful image of the marriage relationship to explain the relationship of Christ to the Church. As a husband is to cherish his wife, to look out for her interests, to aid her in becoming all that God means for her to be, so our Lord nurtures His Church. What this further implies to the husbands is, even as Christ would not torment or abuse His Church, so husbands are never to mistreat their wives. We will circle back around to this in the next chapter.

DISCUSSION QUESTIONS

1) How is submission supposed to work in the marital relationship?

2) How can we keep the idea of submission from being less than God intended?

3) Given what Paul says, how might we advise someone preparing to be married?

26

GOD'S VIEW OF MARRIAGE (PART 2)

EPHESIANS 5:25-32

"Husbands, love your wives, just as Christ loved the church and gave himself up for her to make her holy, cleansing her by the washing with water through the word, and to present her to himself as a radiant church, without stain or wrinkle or any other blemish, but holy and blameless. In this same way, husbands ought to love their wives as their own bodies. He who loves his wife loves himself. After all, no one ever hated their own body, but they feed and care for their body, just as Christ does the church—for we are members of his body. 'For this reason a man will leave his father and mother and be

united to his wife, and the two will become one flesh.' This is a profound mystery—but I am talking about Christ and the church."

If Paul's instructions to wives were not enough, his instructions to husbands were even more revolutionary.

Being a Husband in the Ancient World

In Paul's day it was common for men to be allowed great latitude in their personal conduct as it related to marriage. Initiation of divorce proceedings was entirely in the hands of men and at their whim. Fidelity to wives was optional. Depending on the income level, it was not at all unusual for a man to have a wife to keep his home and bear his children, and then a mistress who met his sexual desires. Rendezvous with other women was totally at the man's behest. While the Jewish faith held much higher standards for marriage, the influx of Gentiles meant that many came in with worldlier assumptions toward marriage.

Love Your Wives

Contrasting the cavalier attitude that many men had toward marriage, Paul counseled husbands to love their wives. Such consideration prevents the physical, emotional, or verbal abuse of their wives. There is no excuse for a man ever to raise his hand in anger against a woman. Too often excuses are made for brutish and aggressive behavior. All people are expected to corral their impulses. Nothing that another person does removes the responsibility for self-control from an individual, nor does a believer have the right to resort to violence, especially against a family member.

A husband loving his wife also means that he is to look after her welfare and as much as possible, meet their needs. This includes financial needs, providing security, intimacy, and sharing in household duties. William Barclay notes, "He must regard her, not as a kind of permanent servant, but as the one person whom it is his duty to cherish."[46]

Equality

But Paul went even further. "… husbands ought to love their wives as their own bodies. He who loves his wife loves himself. After all, no one ever hated their own body, but they feed and care for their body" (vv 28-29). This statement alone flew in the face of all the cultures of the day. While a man might love his wife and cherish her, it was clear to all that *his* needs would always be paramount; that if both were ill, *she* would be the one who would still get up and tend to the household duties while continuing to care for him. She could never rise above this status of second class.

Inspired by the Holy Spirit, Paul insisted that a woman was equal, that her needs were not less than her husband's. In fact, he was to understand that in loving her he was also benefitting. No doubt in the ancient world a Christian marriage stood in stark contrast to other marriages. With the new standard, not only were wives happier, but husbands found themselves happier as they discovered the joys that cannot be known by the self-centered.

Christ and the Church

Throughout this passage Paul not only gave practical instruction on marital relationships, but drew important lessons about how Christ relates to His Church. He reminded them that the Lord Jesus initiated the Church by the laying down of His own life, doing so through a violent and unjust death. Nor did He do so grudgingly but willingly. We who comprise the Bride of Christ look in admiration, spilling into worship at this great act of love that now serves as our example.

The husband "must love as Christ loved the church and gave himself for the church." It must never be a selfish love. "Christ loved the Church, not that the Church might do things for Him but that He might do things for the Church."[47] If a husband ever is unsure of how he should regard his wife, the deeper example of the Church provides the answer. Our Lord would do nothing to harm His Church. Our Lord sustains His Church with His own life. Our Lord provides for His Church in all that it needs. "As a healthy Church is a testimony to our Lord, so a healthy wife is testimony to her husband."

This is the standard for husbands. Husbands who claim to be followers of Christ prove it first within the walls of their own home.

DISCUSSION QUESTIONS

1) How does a healthy or unhealthy marriage reveal the spiritual life of believers?

2) How should a Christian marriage differ from that of unbelievers?

3) "As Christ loved the church." How does that standard line up with the state of your marriage? If you are single, how does this affect the way you approach marriage should that come into your future?

27

CHILDREN AND FATHERS

EPHESIANS 6:1-4

*"Children, obey your parents in the Lord,
for this is right. 'Honor your father and
mother'—which is the first commandment
with a promise—'so that it may go well
with you and that you may enjoy long life
on the earth.' Fathers, do not exasperate
your children; instead, bring them up in the
training and instruction of the Lord."*

The Blessing of Children

Children are, and have always been, considered a
gift from God. To be childless in biblical times was
the same as being cursed, the blame always resting

on the wife for what was considered her failure. On the other hand, to have a lot of children was to be particularly blessed. "Like arrows in the hands of a warrior are children born in one's youth. Blessed is the man whose quiver is full of them" (Psalm 127:4-5).

While children were a joy in themselves, they also served several practical functions in the ancient world. A male child was important as the heir and the one to carry forward the family name. To a poor family, children soon became laborers in the field or workers in the shop. And with no pension system, children ensured that the elderly would be taken care of when they could no longer work.

Harsh Life of Children

While there was benefit to having children, childhood could be harsh. Infant mortality claimed half of children born before their first birthday. Disease, famine, and drought often took younger children first. In the Greek and Roman cultures, children with birth defects or even born the "wrong" gender were left out in the open to be the victims of the cold or the prey of roaming animals.

Fathers had absolute authority over life and death of their children (the mothers had no say). In Roman law, a father could kill or have his child killed with impunity. Because of economic reality, children could, and often were, sold into slavery to settle debts or provide support for a family. In status, they were just above slaves.

Children had no rights. They were expected to not speak until spoken to and to obey without question. While most parents certainly cherished their children and readily sacrificed for them, as it is today, there were parents whose abusive manner marred their children's lives. No one could intercede for a child—he had no recourse but to take it or run away to a place where he might face even crueler treatment or exploitation.

Children in the Christian Household

The elevation of the status of children was seen in the very fact that Paul addressed remarks to them. In these days, everything filtered through the father. That children were noticed and addressed directly was groundbreaking. When the letter was read, no doubt there was a hush in the crowd, perhaps a pause, to take this shift in how family life was to be viewed and practiced.

The obedience demanded of children was fully expected. What was interesting is that Paul did not base that obedience on the demands of culture or even the father's authority but on the command of God accompanied by a promise. "'Honor your father and mother'—which is the first commandment with a promise— 'so that it may go well with you and that you may enjoy long life on the earth'" (vv 2-3).

Paul quotes the fifth commandment but with a twist. In the original it says, "Honor your father and your mother, so that you may live long in the land the Lord your God is giving you" (Exodus 20:12). In the original rendering of the commandment, those who obey the commandment are promised that if they do, "you may live long in the land the Lord your God is giving you." That guarantee was connected to the Promised Land but solely for the Jewish people, and did not pass on to the Church, unlike the spiritual promises. Paul changed it to a more universal meaning: "… so that it may go well with you and that you may enjoy long life on the earth." Either way, heeding this commandment has blessings that will reverberate throughout a person's life.

While a child may have her parents' approval and blessing for obeying, in the Christian life an obedience also brings God's blessing as well. He is taking note of even a child's actions.

Instructions to Parents

If addressing the children was shocking, then the

fathers being told how to parent was even more so. To tell someone how to raise or treat their children would likely be responded to with the ancient equivalent of "mind your own business." But Paul cannot leave them out of the equation. Every member of the household has obligations. It is worth noting here that in Hebrews 11:23, this same word translated to "fathers" refers to both parents, so mothers and fathers are in view.[48]

Because harsh treatment of children was common, limits were put in place for the fathers. They are told, "Do not exasperate your children" (v 4). Holmes notes, "The word 'exasperate' means to 'make angry or resentful.'"[49] In the course of family life, what should be loving can too often become contentious. Although there will no doubt be flareups from time to time, what cannot exist is a bitterness that results in family members provoking one another or seeking moments to embarrass or harass. While such pettiness between children is irksome, it is totally out of place for a parent to act this way toward a child. Children are still impressionable and easily hurt. Since a parent's approval and love is so vital to a child, for a parent to act as an enemy is incredibly harmful.

Counteracting this is what parents were to do

regarding their children. "Bring them up in the training and instruction of the Lord (v 4). This was one of the practices grounded in the Jewish faith that came over into the Christian faith. "These commandments that I give you today are to be on your hearts. Impress them on your children. Talk about them when you sit at home and when you walk along the road, when you lie down and when you get up" (Deuteronomy 6:6-7).

Too often, loving parents provide for their children's physical needs, their education, and their mental wellbeing while starving them of the spiritual instruction and example that they desperately need to become the whole people God intends them to be. It is not enough to take them to church where other people instruct them. They need to hear it, see it, and experience it in the home. Yes, children are to obey. But as parents, we are to instruct.

DISCUSSION QUESTIONS

1) How has Christianity raised the status of children?

2) Why is obedience such a key command for children?

3) Were you raised in a family where God's instruction was in the home? Are you practicing this in your home? Why or why not?

28

SERVICE THAT GLORIFIES GOD

EPHESIANS 6:5-9

*"Slaves, obey your earthly masters with respect
and fear, and with sincerity of heart, just as
you would obey Christ. Obey them not only to
win their favor when their eye is on you, but
as slaves of Christ, doing the will of God from
your heart. Serve wholeheartedly, as if you
were serving the Lord, not people, because you
know that the Lord will reward each one for
whatever good they do, whether they are slave
or free. And masters, treat your slaves in the
same way. Do not threaten them, since you know
that he who is both their Master and yours is in
heaven, and there is no favoritism with him."*

What it Meant to be a First-Century Slave

While bearing important differences from slavery in the more recent past, the life of a slave in the Roman Empire was often agonizing. Unlike the slavery that existed in the British Empire, European nations, and in the United States, slavery was not based on race in ancient days. Anyone could be a slave. People became slaves for a host of reasons: as prisoners of war, thieves making restitution, children sold by their parents, debtors who could not repay what they owed, children born of enslaved parents, those already in slavery but sold to someone else. Slaves had no rights and as far as the Roman law was concerned, were non-persons. They occupied the lowest spot on the social ladder, although some were well educated and had been powerful prior to being enslaved. Slaves served in the military, were doctors and teachers, as well as prostitutes, household servants, and farm laborers.

Because of their lack of status, slaves had no legal recourse for any harm that came to them. Masters were free to kill their slaves or to treat them in the most inhumane way without any legal repercussions. The way slaves were treated depended on the whims of their masters. Some were treated as trusted friends while others just longed to be treated as well as farm animals. "The slave is not better than a beast who happens to talk."[50]

The Roman Empire, as well as its predecessors, relied heavily on slaves to make its economy work, which is the largest reason the institution continued for millennia. At the time of the New Testament, as far as we can estimate, slaves comprised up to thirty percent of the total population, roughly equivalent to the percentage of slaves in the Confederate States at the outbreak of the Civil War.[51] Despite its prevalence and inherent inhumanity, no one in Paul's day questioned the morality of slavery. Nonetheless, as we will see, Paul's instruction to masters in 6:9 radically transforms it, dramatically upending the status quo.

Slaves in the Church

As has happened throughout history, the disenfranchised are often the ones most open to the gospel. Slaves represented many converts in the early Church. While they could not shed their shackles, they could find freedom from their sins.

Oftentimes slaves were first converted, then their masters. As it was, a slave in the local church might hold a position of authority over his master, a new believer. Also, if both master and slave were Christians, it changed the relationship from owner and property to brothers and sisters in Christ. Although some fault the New Testament for not condemning slavery outright, if it had done so, the Church would most surely have been totally wiped out for open sedition. The Roman Empire was none too subtle in the ways it crushed slave revolts and how it punished rebellious slaves. However, in the fellowship of the Church, the institution of slavery began to erode as the love between Christians spilled over into all relationships, including that of master and slave.

But this changeover was not without its challenges. Would a slave exploit her new relationship in Christ to give less service, hoping that her mistress might be more lenient? Would a master exploit his slave based on their brotherhood in Christ to expect more than was warranted?

Household Code: Slaves

This reality demanded definition. Paul instructed slaves to obey their masters, not with a complaining or grudging spirit, but respectfully and sincerely. He warned that their obedience was not to be something to curry favor but was representative of their service to Christ. He stated, "Serve wholeheartedly, as if you were serving the Lord, not people" (v 7).

As he had with children, Paul told slaves to elevate their gaze to an authority higher even than their master. There is a reward for doing good works, whether enslaved or free. "You know that the Lord will reward each one for whatever good they do, whether they are slave or free" (v 8). Not all masters were believers. It didn't matter. Not all believing masters were always fair. It didn't matter. What mattered was what the slave chose to do in his or her heart as a follower of Jesus Christ. Thus, even in slavery, the holy freedom of a believer to be who God intended her to be is preserved. By committing to serve others in Jesus' name, the slave could find a measure of her autonomy restored because she was accountable, not to her earthly master, but to her risen King. No slaveholder could take that away.

It may seem difficult to see how this passage could have any application for us today. However, we can be inspired by the example of the Christian slave in Paul's day and the example of others today who serve the Lord in far more difficult contexts than our own. We can remember that our service, wherever we might be engaged, is viewed by the Lord we serve. Our efforts might not be appreciated. Someone else may take credit for what we have done. It might be difficult, and we might be underpaid. We may even contend with oppression of another sort, if not slavery. Those are realities and are often unjust. Yet, even in the face of such circumstances and even oppression, our ability to choose Christ is not deterred. We can be inspired by Christians who preceded us and found in the Lord the strength to do what is most revolutionary: to love. Living out of the overflow of God's love within us is always an act of defiance in a world consumed by hostility to that same love. Yet, there is a reward awaiting us. The King of kings and the Lord of lords has promised it is so. He is faithful, and His promises are true.

Household Code: Masters

Remembering that in the Roman Empire slaves were of no account. Paul's addressing masters about their obligations represented yet another revolutionary impact of Christianity. Masters are commanded to do the same things to their slaves. Because, Paul reminded them, that as believers they too have a Master. And "there is no favoritism with him" (v 9). On this side of Heaven, the masters enjoyed a more favored position but what their station in life was had no bearing on what their standing would be in eternity. In requiring masters to do the same things as their slaves, Paul was removing from its core the system of privilege that made slavery possible and inserting instead the principle of mutual submission seen throughout the letter. As equal brothers in Christ, the slave would not only look to the needs of his master, but the master would look also to the needs of the slave, considering his slave as more important than himself (Phil. 2:3).

Again, we can find such exhortations instructive today. If one is placed in a position of authority, she must realize that she is to model Christ's example in every area of life. Just as Jesus did not come to be served but to serve, leaders should also seek to serve those under their leadership. Additionally, when Christian leaders fail to measure up to this standard, they can and should be challenged, then given the opportunity to repent and improve. The conduct of the one in a position of authority marks their witness of the Lord they claim as Savior. Lastly, while Paul's words do not directly condemn slavery as an institution, they do provide the basis for doing so. Systems, like slavery, that oppress, harm, and denigrate God's image-bearers are not of the Lord. Paul has been criticized for not more vocally opposing slavery, however, his instruction here and across his letters is the seed that eventually grew into its unraveling. Indeed, it was not long until early Christians were freeing slaves, or, in the case of Gregory of Nyssa, offering perhaps the first denunciation in human history of slavery as inherently evil.

When Times are Unclear, Persevere

Serving the Lord by serving others can often be challenging and sometimes seemingly impossible. It can be difficult to know if our efforts are having any impact at all, if they are truly making a difference. Holmes shares the following illustration: "Several years ago, the cleaning of Michelangelo's frescoes on the ceiling of the Sistine Chapel was undertaken. As the workers carefully removed the buildup of dirt and stain accumulated over the centuries, they marveled at some of the treasures the grime had hidden. Among these unseen portions of the paintings were fingerprints of the artist unnoticed through time. Now they stood in testimony of the artist's identity. Here was the evidence that the master artist had done the work. A part of his identity remained with the product. What fingerprints of our lives do we allow as evidence of our work?"[52]

DISCUSSION QUESTIONS

1) How does sharing the Christian faith with other people form our relationships?

2) How do the rules for slaves toward their masters translate to being an employee? What is different?

3) How do the rules for masters toward slaves translate to someone who is a boss? What is different?

29

SPIRITUAL WARFARE (PART 1)

EPHESIANS 6:10-13

"Finally, be strong in the Lord and in his mighty power. Put on the full armor of God, so that you can take your stand against the devil's schemes. For our struggle is not against flesh and blood, but against the rulers, against the authorities, against the powers of this dark world and against the spiritual forces of evil in the heavenly realms. Therefore put on the full armor of God, so that when the day of evil comes, you may be able to stand your ground, and after you have done everything, to stand."

Pitched Battle in Ephesus

The salvation assault on Ephesus could hardly have been more dramatic. The city boasted the Temple of Diana (see Introduction) that was dubbed one of the Seven Wonders of the Ancient World.[53] Already a major port city, its crowded streets were made more so by the temple that attracted pilgrims from across the Empire, fueling the local economy. For this bastion of pagan worship, Christianity made a frontal assault. Paul labored there for three years, making it the longest continuous ministry he had anywhere. The believers witnessed boldly, "so that all the Jews and Greeks who lived in the province of Asia heard the word of the Lord" (Acts 19:10).

Miracles accompanied the spoken witness, including incredible acts of healing (Acts 19:11–12), and a dramatic case of demons being cast out (Acts 19:13–16). This resulted in many who practiced magic abandoning it in favor of becoming Christians. They witnessed to their conversion by making a public display, burning their books and scrolls devoted to magic (Acts 19:18-19).

But then came the counterattack. As conversions grew, the followers of Diana decreased, so much so that the silversmiths who crafted miniature likenesses of the goddess instigated a riot that left the city in an uproar (Acts 19:23–41). In Ephesus, spiritual warfare was not a vague concept but the stuff of everyday discipleship.

Be Strong

No wonder Paul urged the Ephesians to "be strong in the Lord and in his mighty power" (v 10). Battle is not for the weak of heart or the ones not willing to exert every effort to defeat the enemy. Fortunately, we are not left to our resources nor our own devices. We are to be strong "in his mighty power" (v 10). As one commentator points out, "God doesn't parcel out His power. He gives Himself to His children."[54] We need not fear fatigue if God's power is surging through our spirit.

Put on the Full Armor

In the next few verses Paul both describes the battlefield and what God has provided for us to fight the battle.

We are to "put on the full armor of God" (v 11). The word for "full armor" in Greek is *panoplians*, from which we get the English word "panoply." Its primary meaning has changed very little for it means a complete covering, the total armor from head to foot.[55] God provides all we need to meet the enemy with all means of attack.

This allows believers to "take [their] stand against the devil's schemes" (v 11). By schemes, we mean the devil's strategies, weapons, and skills. The Church Father Chrysostom helpfully points out, "The devil never openly lays temptation before us. He does not mention idolatry out loud. But by this stratagem he presents idolatrous choices to us, by persuasive words and by employing clever euphemisms."[56]

We cannot fail to take the devil seriously. He would like for us to make him the thing of myth or some red-suited character with a pointed tail. Although God provides all we need to defeat Satan, we cannot defeat him if we fail to be on our guard or do not employ the weapons at our disposal. Our armor is not to be dragged out for ceremonial show or on special occasions. It is to be worn and employed every moment of our existence.

The Battlefield

"For our struggle is not against flesh and blood, but against the rulers, against the authorities, against the powers of this dark world and against the spiritual forces of evil in the heavenly realms" (v 12). The battlefield is not just those tangible things in front of us, what we can pick up with our hands.

The battle extends into the spirit realm, far more real than the object you now hold in your hands.

The word for "struggle" is not like our present warfare of distant missile launches or of unseen drones blasting an unsuspecting enemy. Rather, it was hand-to-hand fighting where enemies looked each other in the eye, where they felt the tension in their muscles and their breath as they were near in mortal combat. They saw the blood drawn by their weapons; they heard the breaking of bones.

This passage speaks of ranks of evil. Jewish theology at this time had a well-developed idea of the spirit world, with ranks upon ranks of angels and demons. So prevalent were demons that the Jews taught you could not stick a pin into the air without piercing one. World rulers were under their influence and in their service, not a hard thing to believe when in Paul's day an emperor declared himself to be a god as he ascended the throne.

Believers are to realize that the battle is waged in every phase of life, in every place and time they might be, against an enemy that might in one minute be represented by someone standing in front of us or completely unseen in the spirit world. It is daunting to say the least.

Take Your Stand

Given all this, don't go another minute without ensuring that you are wearing this complete armor. It is the believer's only hope in this vicious battle.

It is interesting that Paul does not command the Christians to advance but rather to stand. He says, "… stand your ground, and after you have done everything, to stand" (v 13). The command to stand is ordered twice in the same sentence, stressing the urgency of holding the ground.

The Roman army perfected a method of battle for its infantry called the *phalanx*. Soldiers clustered together, their shields interlocking with their spears pointed toward the enemy. It was the ancient equivalent to a tank as it pushed the hordes back while protecting the soldiers. But it was equally useful in repelling a charging enemy whose assaults frequently failed as it came up against not only shields and spears, but the combined strength of the soldiers as they stood their ground together.

Note that there is no armor for the back of the soldier. We were meant to conquer— not to retreat. Nor is there any thought that any person is exempt from the combat.

When the Civil War broke out in the United States, one of the opening battles became known as the First Battle of Bull Run. Just outside Washington, D.C., crowds of spectators arrayed themselves on the hillsides to watch the battle in much the same spirit they would attend a theater performance. But this was war and soon the armies spread further as they sought to better each other. The hillsides of spectators became part of the battlefield and those not prepared for battle were thrown into a panic. If any believer thinks this is someone else's battle to fight, he will soon find himself not observing a show but thrown into panic as the enemy attempts his assault.

DISCUSSION QUESTIONS

1) In what ways did ancient Ephesus parallel the twenty-first century?

2) In what ways do you see the Christian life as a battle?

3) What does the Bible mean when it says, "spiritual forces of evil in the heavenly realms"?

30

SPIRITUAL WARFARE (PART 2)

EPHESIANS 6:14-18

"Stand firm then, with the belt of truth buckled around your waist, with the breastplate of righteousness in place, and with your feet fitted with the readiness that comes from the gospel of peace. In addition to all this, take up the shield of faith, with which you can extinguish all the flaming arrows of the evil one. Take the helmet of salvation and the sword of the Spirit, which is the word of God. And pray in the Spirit on all occasions with all kinds of prayers and requests. With this in mind, be alert and always keep on praying for all the Lord's people."

Stand

After having told the Ephesians to stand, Paul repeated the command again. Why would he say this yet again? Because he knew how easy it was for people to fall or to retreat from the battle. The opposition that flared up against the believers in Ephesus (Acts 19) was not the end of the conflict but the opening salvos of a long and difficult war. The enemy would continue to assail the gates of Christianity, not only in Ephesus but in Corinth, Jerusalem, Rome, London, New York City, and Tokyo. It was not to be a one-day skirmish but siege warfare, across the miles and over the centuries. The only hope was for believers not to fall away or retreat. They had to boldly face the enemy wherever he might attack and with whatever weapons he employed. "Stand firm," says Paul, not just to the Ephesians but to you in this day's battle; to you wherever that battlefield is; to you whether outnumbered or standing in a host of allies. Stand firm.

Belt of Truth

The belt held the soldier's tunic in place and was where his sword hung. Its main purpose was to allow for freedom of movement so that the soldier was able to turn in an instant to face the enemy.[58]

For the believer, it is to know what truth is, and for us the ultimate truth is found in God's revealed Word. Where God has spoken, there is no place for speculation. To doubt it would be akin to a soldier wearing his belt loose so that it became more of a hindrance than a help.

It is not only knowing the truth but speaking the truth, being authentic. We will be believed if we are believable. What we say in our witness will be given a hearing if we have been trustworthy in other matters. Lying lips betray any testimony to God's power.

Breastplate of Righteousness

The breastplate may have been the most important piece of protective armor. It covered the vital organs, including the lungs, digestive system, heart, pancreas, and liver. A wound to any one of these organs could be fatal or at the very least, seriously disable the warrior. Remember that in ancient times, people believed that thought and emotions were based in the heart—they did not fully understand the function of the brain. We see this in modern day when we speak of someone having a broken heart or similar expressions.

The crafting of a breastplate was of utmost importance. If it was too thin, it failed to protect the soldier. If it was not fitted properly, it could prevent a soldier from being as nimble as he needed to be in battle. It had to be right or it might be useless.

Paul said our breastplate is righteousness (right living or holy living). The person who is living righteously will not participate in things she knows are harmful to her soul. Someone living a holy life will avoid certain places, and filter what he reads and views. This protects the believer.

Holmes observes, "The presence of a breastplate of righteousness reveals the Enemy's propensity to use unrighteousness to destroy God's people."[59] The Christian is to be prepared with the breastplate of righteousness firmly fitted in place.

Feet with Gospel of Peace

The Roman army took great care in making sure that the feet of its infantry were well protected. They needed footwear that would allow them to march great distances but also give their soldiers a firm footing when the enemy attacked. A slip of the foot could have deadly consequences. The shoes allowed him to be quick, ready to move, and keep his balance on rough terrain.

Interesting, then, in this discussion of warfare we come across the word "peace." What is this peace?

It is peace with God that gives us a firm footing as we face the battle, that calms our hearts when others might panic. It is a peace that comes when someone who has opposed us yields to the grace of God, and we pull them up to embrace them and call them brothers and sisters.

Shield of Faith

The shield most used by the Romans was the Legionnaire Scutum. It was curved, covered most of the body, and had a small opening that allowed the soldier to see in front of him. It offered great protection for the soldier.[60] Some were made of wood and covered with a thick layer of leather. When flaming arrows hit the shields, they penetrated far enough to suffocate the fire.

The shield of faith shields us against the enemy's attacks. It is both the faith, that is, the set of beliefs that are the core of our Christian beliefs, and the individual faith of the believer that God is able to deliver and to conquer.

Helmet of Salvation

Most of our senses are located in our head: sight, hearing, taste, and smell. Here we receive input from the world around us moment by moment. The senses signal our state of being and give us what we need to act. The loss of any of our senses is disorienting, and while not likely fatal, can compromise our response.

Salvation sets it all right. While loss of our spiritual senses will disorient and compromise our ability to react, salvation tunes our spiritual senses, so that we are saved from condemnation and attuned to what God says to us through His Holy Spirit.

Sword of the Spirit

The Roman sword was relatively short with a blade only about twenty-four inches long. Double-edged, it was meant for close fighting, face-to-face with the enemy. It could be used for defense and offense.

Paul says that the sword of the Spirit is the "word of God" (v 17). That can be understood two ways. First, and the most frequent application, is that it is the Word of God—the Bible. No doubt this is true. God's Word has unassailable authority and changes lives, instructs, and reproves as necessary. Only a foolish Christian ignores his Bible or nibbles on crumbs when he has the whole Bible to feast upon. Nor is it enough to get our serving of Scripture through a third party like a preacher or teacher. We need to get to know the Bible by reading it ourselves.

But "word of God" can also mean our spoken word of testimony. If we are to live the Christian life, it is not to be done with sealed lips. We need to speak for our Lord, trusting Him to use our simple, bumbling words as a sword.

Prayer

Although technically not a weapon or part of the armor, Paul concludes this section with the importance of prayer. Communication between God and us is vital, as communication is vital to the execution of a successful battle. We need to know our Commander's mind, heed His instruction, and move as He instructs. He is the One who sustains us in the day of battle, who teaches us how to fight. Prayer is the vital connection.

DISCUSSION QUESTIONS

1) How does thinking of the Christian life as a battle help you know how to live?

2) Which one of the pieces of armor do you feel you need right now? Why?

3) How do you take your stand for the Lord?

31

FINAL THOUGHTS

EPHESIANS 6:19-24

"Pray also for me, that whenever I speak, words may be given me so that I will fearlessly make known the mystery of the gospel, for which I am an ambassador in chains. Pray that I may declare it fearlessly, as I should. Tychicus, the dear brother and faithful servant in the Lord, will tell you everything, so that you also may know how I am and what I am doing. I am sending him to you for this very purpose, that you may know how we are, and that he may encourage you. Peace to the brothers and sisters, and love with faith from God the Father and the Lord Jesus Christ. Grace to all who love our Lord Jesus Christ with an undying love."

Pray for Me

Commissioner Israel Gaither, retired USA National Commander for The Salvation Army, shared in an interview that one of the ways to instill mission in people is to begin the day with prayer. The interviewer asked, "Can it be that simple? Can everyone stay out of trouble with a morning prayer?" Gaither replied, "I serve in a world weakened by sin. That's the context in which I serve, and I have to ask God to protect me—my mind, my thinking, and my behavior. Is that the path to help an organization do what is right? Yeah. I think that's the way to do it."[61]

As Paul was closing this powerful letter, he humbly asked for the prayers of other believers. No doubt that even at this time he was a towering figure in the Church. His letters helped crystalize the teachings handed down from Christ through the apostles. In them, he formulated successful defenses against error that even then had started to creep into the Church. His word sent people across the Roman Empire and beyond, yet here he meekly asked for the prayers of others. Paul never saw himself as self-sufficient, as having reached some plane of spiritual maturity where he didn't need the prayers of the simplest believer. The Christian life is sustained by prayer, in that place where the eternal God bends forward to hear us whisper in His ear and then speaks back to us in a voice beyond physical ears or hearing.

Paul's Prayer List

As Paul sat in prison, he could have asked believers to pray for his deliverance. But he did not. Shut off from the world, he could have prayed that there would be a parade of visitors to ease his loneliness. But he did not. He would have been underfed, yet he did not pray for food. He would have shivered through the cold nights, but he asked for no blankets. His prayer was that he would be a faithful witness so "that whenever I speak, words may be given me so that I will fearlessly make known the mystery of the gospel" (v 19).

Shut away and set aside, Paul could only think of a lost world that was at that moment starving for the gospel. But even here, when opportunity came, he asked that God give him the words for the moment and the occasion. When you go to the Lord in prayer, does such a request find a place in your petitions?

An Ambassador in Chains

The role of an ambassador has changed little over the centuries. As a representative of his homeland's government in a foreign land, the ambassador speaks on behalf of his country to the highest powers where he serves. Ambassadors have access where others are denied because of the importance of the people they represent and the messages they convey. They have a certain degree of immunity because of their role.

How odd, then, for Paul to claim he was an ambassador—in chains! What ambassador could serve without access to the rulers of a land or from a prison cell? Freedom of movement was key to them fulfilling their responsibilities.

Paul was right. He represented a King, speaking on behalf of Him and for His interests. Chains could not bar Paul from his task. Here is an important lesson that the old Apostle had learned long ago. His service never depended on his circumstance. He might be locked up, shouted down, driven out of cities, and beaten by mobs, but his role remained the same. He was an ambassador, representing the King of kings. No walls or woes could move him from that.

Tychicus

Paul could not come, but Tychicus could. Tychicus, an Asian convert to Christianity, was from nearby Colossae. We do not know a single word he uttered. We know of no great acts he performed or if he ever held any important office. We know he carried messages from Paul to Ephesus and Colossae, and later to Titus.

Tychicus performed well with the task and the opportunity he was given. Perhaps he had aspired to something more. We can never know. What we can discover is that he was faithful with what he was given to do. How do we know? The letters to the Ephesians, Colossians, and to Titus all reached their destination. Faithfulness was proven by the work that was done.

He was more than a postal worker. He carried news of Paul to these places and encouraged the people there. Then he reported back to Paul about how the people were doing. Maybe we can call him a "gospel gossip," not with destructive talk that often makes up gossip, but with words of encouragement to people that showed genuine interest in those he touched.

Peace, Love, and Grace

In customary fashion Paul ended the letter with a blessing of peace, love, and grace, the constant and abiding gifts of the Christian life. There really is nothing better we can wish for and to our brothers and sisters in Christ. These gifts sustain us and give us that scent of Heaven while still anchored to this earth.

DISCUSSION QUESTIONS

1) What is your prayer life like in what you pray and the time you devote to it?

2) As an ambassador of Christ, how well are you representing Him?

3) Why is it important to think about lesser-known biblical characters like Tychicus?

ENDNOTES

1. Mark A. Holmes, *Ephesians* (Indianapolis: Wesleyan Publishing House, 1997), 12.

2. Holmes, 14.

3. Robert F. Youngblood, *Nelson's New Illustrated Bible Dictionary* (Nashville: Nelson, 1995), 406-407.

4. Holmes, 11.

5. Mark J. Edwards, *Ancient Commentary on Scripture, Volume VIII* (Downer's Grove, IL: Inter-Varsity Press, 1999), 104.

6. Hoehner, Harold W. *Ephesians, an Exegetical Commentary*. Baker Academic: Grand Rapids, MI, 2002, 196.

7. *Ibid.*, 198.

8. *Parables, Etc.*, Volume 3, No. 11, January 1984, pg. 4.

9. Tony Merida, *Exalting Jesus in Ephesians* (Nashville: Holman, 2014), 38.

10. Harold W. Hoehner, *Ephesians* (Grand Rapids: Baker Academic, 2002), 283.

11. *Ibid.*, 292.

12. W. A. Criswell, *Ephesians* (Grand Rapids: Zondervan, 1974), 67.

13. Mark J. Edwards, *Ancient Commentary on Scripture* (Chicago: Moody Press, 1999), 123.

14. Barclay, William, *The Letters to the Galatians and Ephesians* (Philadelphia: The Westminster Press, 1958), 122.

15. William Barclay. *The Letters to the Galatians and Ephesians* (Philadelphia: The Westminster Press, 1958), 125.

16. Harold W. Hoehner, *Ephesians* (Grand Rapids: Baker Academic, 2002), 362.

17. https://christiananswers.net/spotlight/movies/2003/

peacechild.html. The movie and book are still available.

18. William Barclay. *The Letters to the Galatians and Ephesians* (Philadelphia: The Westminster Press, 1958), 136.

19. Mark A. Holmes, *Ephesians* (Indianapolis: Wesleyan Publishing House, 1997), 86.

20. William Barclay. *The Letters to the Galatians and Ephesians* (Philadelphia: The Westminster Press, 1958), 142.

21. Tony Evans, *Tony Evans Book of Illustrations*. Moody Publishers: Chicago (2009), pg. 297-298.

22. Craig Brian Larson and Phyllis Ten Elshof. *1001 Illustrations That Connect*. Zondervan: Grand Rapids, MI (2008), pg. 291.

23. Mark A. Holmes, *Ephesians* (Indianapolis: Wesleyan Publishing House, 1997), 104.

24. https://www.azquotes.com/quote/292318.

25. https://library.timelesstruths.org/music/The_Love_of_God/ accessed 2/5/23.

26. William Barclay. *The Letters to the Galatians and Ephesians* (Philadelphia: The Westminster Press, 1958), 160.

27. *Ibid.*, 163.

28. William Barclay. *The Letters to the Galatians and Ephesians* (Philadelphia: The Westminster Press, 1958), 178.

29. Mark A. Holmes, *Ephesians* (Indianapolis: Wesleyan Publishing House, 1997), 128.

30. John R. W. Stott, *The Message of Ephesians* (Downer's Grove, IL: Inter-Varsity Press, 1974), 136.

31. Tony Merida, *Exalting Jesus in Ephesians* (Nashville: Holman, 2014), 106.

32. https://library.timelesstruths.org/music/I_Have_Decided_to_Follow_Jesus/ accessed January 3, 2023.

33. William Barclay. *The Letters to the Galatians and Ephe-*

sians (Philadelphia: The Westminster Press, 1958), 181.

34. Mark J. Edwards, *Ancient Church Commentary on Scripture, Volume VIII* (Downer's Grove, IL: Inter-Varsity Press, 1999), 163.

35. Tony Merida, *Exalting Jesus in Ephesians*, (Nashville: Holman, 2014), 111.

36. Rick Ebell in *One-Minute Uplift*, quoted in *1001 Illustrations that Connect*, Craig Brian Larson and Phyllis Ten Elshof.

37. Tony Merida, *Exalting Jesus in Ephesians* (Nashville: Holman, 2014), 113.

38. Tony Merida, *Exalting Jesus in Ephesians*, (Nashville: Holman, 2014), 121.

39. Kenneth J. Collins & Robert W. Wall, *Wesley One Volume Commentary* (Grand Rapids: William B. Eerdman's Press, 1996), 791.

40. Tony Evans, *Tony Evans Book of Illustrations* (Chicago: Moody Press, 2009), 184.

41. https://www.cdc.gov/alcohol/features/excessive-drinking.html, accessed January 26, 2023.

42. https://recoverycentersofamerica.com/resource/economic-cost-of-substance-abuse-disorder-in-united-states-2019/ accessed January 26, 2023.

43. http://www.sermonillustrations.com/a-z/m/marriage.htm Accessed 1/26/23.

44. Karen H. Jobes, *1 Peter* (Grand Rapids, IL: Baker Academic, 2005), 203.

45. William Barclay, *The Letters of James and Peter* (Philadelphia: The Westminster Press, 1960), 260.

46. William Barclay, *The Letters to the Galatians and Ephesians* (Philadelphia: The Westminster Press, 1958), 205.

47. William Barclay, *The Letters to the Galatians and Ephesians* (Philadelphia: The Westminster Press, 1958), 205-206.

48. Tony Merida, *Exalting Jesus in Ephesians* (Nashville: Holman, 2014), 151.

49. Mark A. Holmes, *Ephesians* (Indianapolis: Wesleyan Publishing House, 1997), 179.

50. Barclay.

51. https://www.historyguy.com/civilwar/statistics_slave_population.html accessed 1/28/23.

52. Mark A. Holmes, *Ephesians* (Indianapolis: Wesleyan Publishing House, 1999), 184.

53. Ronald Youngblood, *New Illustrated Bible Dictionary*.

54. Charles W. Carter, *The Wesleyan Bible Commentary, Volume 5* (Nashville: Abingdon Press, 1965), 434.

55. William Barclay, *The Letters to the Galatians and Ephesians* (Philadelphia: The Westminster Press, 1958), 216.

56. Mark J. Edwards, *Ancient Commentary on Scripture* (Downer's Grove, IL: Inter-Varsity Press, 1999), 197.

58. William Barclay, *The Letters to the Galatians and Ephesians* (Philadelphia: The Westminster Press, 1958), 217.

59. Mark A. Holmes, *Ephesians* (Indianapolis: Wesleyan Publishing House, 1999), 191.

60. https://www.historyhit.com/kinds-of-ancient-roman-shields/ accessed 2/3/23.

61. Del Jones, "Salvation Army's Chief on a Mission," *USA Today* (November 20, 2006).

BIBLIOGRAPHY

Barclay, William. *The Letters to the Galatians and Ephesians* (Philadelphia: The Westminster Press, 1958).

Collins, Kenneth J. & Wall, Robert W., Editors, *Wesley One Volume Commentary* (Nashville: Abingdon Press, 2020).

Criswell, W. A. *Ephesians* (Grand Rapids: Zondervan, 1974).

Carter, Charles W. *The Wesleyan Bible Commentary, Volume 5* (Grand Rapids: William B. Eerdman's Press, 1965).

Donelson, Lewis R. *Colossians, Ephesians, 1 and 2 Timothy and Titus* (Louisville: West Minster John Knox Press, 1996).

Edwards, Mark J. *Ancient Christian Commentary on Scripture, Volume VIII* (Downer's Grove, IL: Inter-Varsity Press, 1999).

Evans, Tony. *Tony Evans' Book of Illustrations* (Chicago: Moody Press, 2009).

Green, Michael P. *1500 Illustrations for Biblical Preaching* (Grand Rapids: Baker Books, 1989).

Hoehner, Harold W. *Ephesians* (Grand Rapids: Baker Academic, 2002).

Holmes, Mark A. *Ephesians* (Indianapolis: Wesleyan Publishing House, 1997).

Jobes, Karen H. *1 Peter* (Grand Rapids, IL: Baker Academic, 2005).

Larson, Craig Brian. *750 Engaging Illustrations* (Grand Rapids: Baker Books, 2002).

Larson, Craig Brian & Ten Elshof, Phyllis, General Editors. *1001 Illustrations that Connect* (Grand Rapids: Christianity Today International, 2008).

Merida, Tony. *Exalting Jesus in Ephesians* (Nashville: Holman, 2014).

Morgan, Robert J. *Preacher's Sourcebook of Creative Sermon Illustrations* (Nashville: Thomas Nelson Publishers, 2007).

Stott, John R. W. *The Message of Ephesians* (Downer's Grove, IL: Inter-Varsity Press, 1974).

Taylor, Willard H. *Beacon Bible Commentary, Volume IX* (Kansas City: Beacon Press, 1965).

Witherington, Ben III. *The Letters to Philemon, the Colossians and the Ephesians* (Grand Rapids: William B. Eerdman's Press, 2007).

Wright, N.T. *Paul, the Prison Letters* (Louisville: John Knox Press, 2004).

Youngblood, Ronald F., General Editor. *New Illustrated Bible Dictionary* (Nashville: Thomas Nelson Publishers, 1995).